O9-CFU-207

DISCARDED

COLLEGE OF THE SEQUOIAS
LIBRARY

NUCLEAR MEDICINE

COLLEGE OF THE SEQUOIAS

LIBRARY

GENERAL EDITORS

Dale C. Garell, M.D.
Medical Director, California Children Services, Department of Health Services,
    County of Los Angeles
Associate Dean for Curriculum; Clinical Professor, Department of Pediatrics &
    Family Medicine, University of Southern California School of Medicine
Former President, Society for Adolescent Medicine

Solomon H. Snyder, M.D.
Distinguished Service Professor of Neuroscience, Pharmacology, and Psychiatry, Johns
    Hopkins University School of Medicine
Former President, Society for Neuroscience
Albert Lasker Award in Medical Research, 1978

CONSULTING EDITORS

Robert W. Blum, M.D., Ph.D.
Professor and Director, Division of General Pediatrics and Adolescent Health,
    University of Minnesota

Charles E. Irwin, Jr., M.D.
Professor of Pediatrics; Director, Division of Adolescent Medicine, University of California, San Francisco

Lloyd J. Kolbe, Ph.D.
Director of the Division of Adolescent and School Health, Center for Chronic
    Disease Prevention and Health Promotion, Centers for Disease Control

Jordan J. Popkin
Former Director, Division of Federal Employee Occupational Health, U.S. Public
    Health Service Region I

Joseph L. Rauh, M.D.
Professor of Pediatrics and Medicine, Adolescent Medicine, Children's Hospital
    Medical Center, Cincinnati
Former President, Society for Adolescent Medicine

THE ENCYCLOPEDIA OF
HEALTH

MEDICAL DISORDERS
AND THEIR TREATMENT

Dale C. Garell, M.D. · General Editor

NUCLEAR MEDICINE

Wendy and Jack Murphy

Introduction by C. Everett Koop, M.D., Sc.D.

former Surgeon General, U. S. Public Health Service

CHELSEA HOUSE PUBLISHERS

New York · Philadelphia

The goal of the ENCYCLOPEDIA OF HEALTH *is to provide general information in the ever-changing areas of physiology, psychology, and related medical issues. The titles in this series are not intended to take the place of the professional advice of a physician or other health care professional.*

ON THE COVER A technician prepares his computer monitor while, in the background, a patient is readied for a CT scan

CHELSEA HOUSE PUBLISHERS
EDITORIAL DIRECTOR   Richard Rennert
EXECUTIVE MANAGING EDITOR   Karyn Gullen Browne
EXECUTIVE EDITOR   Sean Dolan
COPY CHIEF   Robin James
PICTURE EDITOR   Adrian G. Allen
ART DIRECTOR   Robert Mitchell
MANUFACTURING DIRECTOR   Gerald Levine
SYSTEMS MANAGER   Lindsey Ottman
PRODUCTION COORDINATOR   Marie Claire Cebrián-Ume

The Encyclopedia of Health
SENIOR EDITOR   Don Nardo

Staff for NUCLEAR MEDICINE
EDITORIAL ASSISTANT   Mary B. Sisson
PICTURE RESEARCHER   Sandy Jones
DESIGNER   M. Cambraia Magalhães

Copyright © 1994 by Chelsea House Publishers, a division of Main Line Book Co. All rights reserved. Printed and bound in the United States of America.

First Printing
1   3   5   7   9   8   6   4   2

Library of Congress Cataloging-in-Publication Data

Murphy, Wendy B.
   Nuclear Medicine/Wendy and Jack Murphy
      p. cm.—(The Encyclopedia of health. Medical disorders and their treatment)
   Includes bibliographical references and index.
Summary: Reviews the history of nuclear medicine beginning with the discovery of the X ray and follows the evolution of the field to the present, using specific medical problems in examples of how the technology works.
ISBN 0-7910-0070-2
      0-7910-0497-X (pbk.)
   1. Nuclear medicine—Juvenile literature. 2. Radiography, Medical—Juvenile litera-ture. [1. Nuclear medicine. 2. Radiology, Medical.] I. Murphy, Jack (Jack J.) II. Title. III. Series.
R895.M87 1994   92-44342
616.07'57—dc20   CIP
                                                                                                        AC

CONTENTS

THE ENCYCLOPEDIA OF
H E A L T H

THE HEALTHY BODY

The Circulatory System
Dental Health
The Digestive System
The Endocrine System
Exercise
Genetics & Heredity
The Human Body: An Overview
Hygiene
The Immune System
Memory & Learning
The Musculoskeletal System
The Nervous System
Nutrition
The Reproductive System
The Respiratory System
The Senses
Sleep
Speech & Hearing
Sports Medicine
Vision
Vitamins & Minerals

THE LIFE CYCLE

Adolescence
Adulthood
Aging
Childhood
Death & Dying
The Family
Friendship & Love
Pregnancy & Birth

MEDICAL ISSUES

Careers in Health Care
Environmental Health
Folk Medicine
Health Care Delivery
Holistic Medicine
Medical Ethics
Medical Fakes & Frauds
Medical Technology
Medicine & the Law
Occupational Health
Public Health

PSYCHOLOGICAL DISORDERS AND THEIR TREATMENT

Anxiety & Phobias
Child Abuse
Compulsive Behavior
Delinquency & Criminal Behavior
Depression
Diagnosing & Treating Mental Illness
Eating Habits & Disorders
Learning Disabilities
Mental Retardation
Personality Disorders
Schizophrenia
Stress Management
Suicide

MEDICAL DISORDERS AND THEIR TREATMENT

AIDS
Allergies
Alzheimer's Disease
Arthritis
Birth Defects
Cancer
The Common Cold
Diabetes
Emergency Medicine
Gynecological Disorders
Headaches
The Hospital
Kidney Disorders
Medical Diagnosis
The Mind-Body Connection
Mononucleosis and Other Infectious Diseases
Nuclear Medicine
Organ Transplants
Pain
Physical Handicaps
Poisons & Toxins
Prescription & OTC Drugs
Sexually Transmitted Diseases
Skin Disorders
Stroke & Heart Disease
Substance Abuse
Tropical Medicine

PREVENTION AND EDUCATION: THE KEYS TO GOOD HEALTH

C. Everett Koop, M.D., Sc.D.
former Surgeon General,
U.S. Public Health Service

The issue of health education has received particular attention in recent years because of the presence of AIDS in the news. But our response to this particular tragedy points up a number of broader issues that doctors, public health officials, educators, and the public face. In particular, it points up the necessity for sound health education for citizens of all ages.

Over the past 25 years this country has been able to bring about dramatic declines in the death rates for heart disease, stroke, accidents, and for people under the age of 45, cancer. Today, Americans generally eat better and take better care of themselves than ever before. Thus, with the help of modern science and technology, they have a better chance of surviving serious—even catastrophic—illnesses. That's the good news.

But, like every phonograph record, there's a flip side, and one with special significance for young adults. According to a report issued in 1979 by Dr. Julius Richmond, my predecessor as Surgeon General, Americans aged 15 to 24 had a higher death rate in 1979 than they did 20 years earlier. The causes: violent death and injury, alcohol and drug abuse, unwanted pregnancies, and sexually transmitted diseases. Adolescents are particularly vulnerable because they are beginning to explore their own sexuality and perhaps to experiment with drugs. The need for educating young people is critical, and the price of neglect is high.

Yet even for the population as a whole, our health is still far from what it could be. Why? A 1974 Canadian government report attributed all death and disease to four broad elements: inadequacies in the health care system, behavioral factors or unhealthy life-styles, environmental hazards, and human biological factors.

To be sure, there are diseases that are still beyond the control of even our advanced medical knowledge and techniques. And despite yearnings that are as old as the human race itself, there is no "fountain of youth" to ward off aging and death. Still, there is a solution to many of the problems that undermine sound health. In a word, that solution is prevention. Prevention, which includes health promotion and education, saves lives, improves the quality of life, and in the long run, saves money.

In the United States, organized public health activities and preventive medicine have a long history. Important milestones in this country or foreign breakthroughs adopted in the United States include the improvement of sanitary procedures and the development of pasteurized milk in the late 19th century and the introduction in the mid-20th century of effective vaccines against polio, measles, German measles, mumps, and other once-rampant diseases. Internationally, organized public health efforts began on a wide-scale basis with the International Sanitary Conference of 1851, to which 12 nations sent representatives. The World Health Organization, founded in 1948, continues these efforts under the aegis of the United Nations, with particular emphasis on combating communicable diseases and the training of health care workers.

Despite these accomplishments, much remains to be done in the field of prevention. For too long, we have had a medical care system that is science- and technology-based, focused, essentially, on illness and mortality. It is now patently obvious that both the social and the economic costs of such a system are becoming insupportable.

Implementing prevention—and its corollaries, health education and promotion—is the job of several groups of people.

First, the medical and scientific professions need to continue basic scientific research, and here we are making considerable progress. But increased concern with prevention will also have a decided impact on how primary care doctors practice medicine. With a shift to health-based rather than morbidity-based medicine, the role of the "new physician" will include a healthy dose of patient education.

Second, practitioners of the social and behavioral sciences—psychologists, economists, city planners—along with lawyers, business leaders, and government officials—must solve the practical and ethical dilemmas confronting us: poverty, crime, civil rights, literacy, education, employment, housing, sanitation, environmental protection, health care delivery systems, and so forth. All of these issues affect public health.

Third is the public at large. We'll consider that very important group in a moment.

Fourth, and the linchpin in this effort, is the public health profession—doctors, epidemiologists, teachers—who must harness the professional expertise of the first two groups and the common sense and cooperation of the third, the public. They must define the problems statistically and qualitatively and then help us set priorities for finding the solutions.

To a very large extent, improving those statistics is the responsibility of every individual. So let's consider more specifically what the role of the individual should be and why health education is so important to that role. First, and most obvious, individuals can protect themselves from illness and injury and thus minimize their need for professional medical care. They can eat nutritious food; get adequate exercise; avoid tobacco, alcohol, and drugs; and take prudent steps to avoid accidents. The proverbial "apple a day keeps the doctor away" is not so far from the truth, after all.

Second, individuals should actively participate in their own medical care. They should schedule regular medical and dental checkups. Should they develop an illness or injury, they should know when to treat themselves and when to seek professional help. To gain the maximum benefit from any medical treatment that they do require, individuals must become partners in that treatment. For instance, they should understand the effects and side effects of medications. I counsel young physicians that there is no such thing as too much information when talking with patients. But the corollary is the patient must know enough about the nuts and bolts of the healing process to understand what the doctor is telling him or her. That is at least partially the patient's responsibility.

Education is equally necessary for us to understand the ethical and public policy issues in health care today. Sometimes individuals will encounter these issues in making decisions about their own treatment or that of family members. Other citizens may encounter them as jurors in medical malpractice cases. But we all become involved, indirectly, when we elect our public officials, from school board members to the president. Should surrogate parenting be legal? To what extent is drug testing desirable, legal, or necessary? Should there be public funding for family planning, hospitals, various types of medical research, and other medical care for the indigent? How should we allocate scant technological resources, such as kidney dialysis and organ transplants? What is the proper role of government in protecting the rights of patients?

What are the broad goals of public health in the United States today? In 1980, the Public Health Service issued a report aptly entitled *Promoting Health—Preventing Disease: Objectives for the Nation*. This report expressed its goals in terms of mortality and in terms of intermediate goals in education and health improvement. It identified 15 major concerns: controlling high blood pressure; improving family planning; improving pregnancy care and infant health; increasing the rate of immunization; controlling sexually transmitted diseases; controlling the presence of toxic agents and radiation in the environment; improving occupational safety and health; preventing accidents; promoting water fluoridation and dental health; controlling infectious diseases; decreasing smoking; decreasing alcohol and drug abuse; improving nutrition; promoting physical fitness and exercise; and controlling stress and violent behavior.

For healthy adolescents and young adults (ages 15 to 24), the specific goal was a 20% reduction in deaths, with a special focus on motor vehicle injuries and alcohol and drug abuse. For adults (ages 25 to 64), the aim was 25% fewer deaths, with a concentration on heart attacks, strokes, and cancers.

Smoking is perhaps the best example of how individual behavior can have a direct impact on health. Today, cigarette smoking is recognized as the single most important preventable cause of death in our society. It is responsible for more cancers and more cancer deaths than any other known agent; is a prime risk factor for heart and blood vessel disease, chronic bronchitis, and emphysema; and is a frequent cause of complications in pregnancies and of babies born prematurely, underweight, or with potentially fatal respiratory and cardiovascular problems.

Since the release of the Surgeon General's first report on smoking in 1964, the proportion of adult smokers has declined substantially, from 43% in 1965 to 30.5% in 1985. Since 1965, 37 million people have quit smoking. Although there is still much work to be done if we are to become a "smoke-free society," it is heartening to note that public health and public education efforts—such as warnings on cigarette packages and bans on broadcast advertising—have already had significant effects.

In 1835, Alexis de Tocqueville, a French visitor to America, wrote, "In America the passion for physical well-being is general." Today, as then, health and fitness are front-page items. But with the greater scientific and technological resources now available to us, we are in a far stronger position to make good health care available to everyone. And with the greater technological threats to us as we approach the 21st century, the need to do so is more urgent than ever before. Comprehensive information about basic biology, preventive medicine, medical and surgical treatments, and related ethical and public policy issues can help you arm yourself with the knowledge you need to be healthy throughout your life.

FOREWORD

Dale C. Garell, M.D.

Advances in our understanding of health and disease during the 20th century have been truly remarkable. Indeed, it could be argued that modern health care is one of the greatest accomplishments in all of human history. In the early 20th century, improvements in sanitation, water treatment, and sewage disposal reduced death rates and increased longevity. Previously untreatable illnesses can now be managed with antibiotics, immunizations, and modern surgical techniques. Discoveries in the fields of immunology, genetic diagnosis, and organ transplantation are revolutionizing the prevention and treatment of disease. Modern medicine is even making inroads against cancer and heart disease, two of the leading causes of death in the United States.

Although there is much to be proud of, medicine continues to face enormous challenges. Science has vanquished diseases such as smallpox and polio, but new killers, most notably AIDS, confront us. Moreover, we now victimize ourselves with what some have called "diseases of choice," or those brought on by drug and alcohol abuse, bad eating habits, and mismanagement of the stresses and strains of contemporary life. The very technology that is doing so much to prolong life has brought with it previously unimaginable ethical dilemmas related to issues of death and dying. The rising cost of health care is a matter of central concern to us all. And violence in the form of automobile accidents, homicide, and suicide remains the major killer of young adults.

In the past, most people were content to leave health care and medical treatment in the hands of professionals. But since the 1960s, the consumer of medical care—that is, the patient—has assumed an increasingly central role in the management of his or her own health. There has also been a new emphasis placed on prevention: People are recognizing that their own actions can help prevent many of the conditions that have caused death and disease in the past. This accounts for the growing commitment to good nutrition and regular exercise, for the increasing number of people who are choosing not to smoke, and for a new moderation in people's drinking habits.

People want to know more about themselves and their own health. They are curious about their body: its anatomy, physiology, and biochemistry. They want to keep up with rapidly evolving medical technologies and procedures. They are willing to educate themselves about common disorders and diseases so that they can be full partners in their own health care.

THE ENCYCLOPEDIA OF HEALTH is designed to provide the basic knowledge that readers will need if they are to take significant responsibility for their own health. It is also meant to serve as a frame of reference for further study and exploration. The encyclopedia is divided into five subsections: The Healthy Body; The Life Cycle; Medical Disorders & Their Treatment; Psychological Disorders & Their Treatment; and Medical Issues. For each topic covered by the encyclopedia, we present the essential facts about the relevant biology; the symptoms, diagnosis, and treatment of common diseases and disorders; and ways in which you can prevent or reduce the severity of health problems when that is possible. The encyclopedia also projects what may lie ahead in the way of future treatment or prevention strategies.

The broad range of topics and issues covered in the encyclopedia reflects that human health encompasses physical, psychological, social, environmental, and spiritual well-being. Just as the mind and the body are inextricably linked, so, too, is the individual an integral part of the wider world that comprises his or her family, society, and environment. To discuss health in its broadest aspect it is necessary to explore the many ways in which it is connected to such fields as law, social science, public policy, economics, and even religion. And so, the encyclopedia is meant to be a bridge between science, medical technology, the world at large, and you. I hope that it will inspire you to pursue in greater depth particular areas of interest and that you will take advantage of the suggestions for further reading and the lists of resources and organizations that can provide additional information.

CHAPTER 1

MYSTERIOUS RAYS AND THE BIRTH OF RADIOLOGY

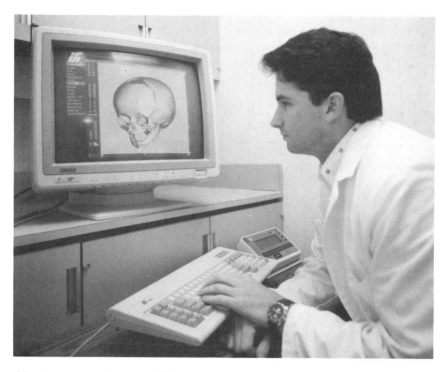

Modern computer graphics programs can translate the data from nuclear diagnostic machines Into pictures that aid doctors in analyzing internal injuries.

Within the past century, science has made living a long and healthy life possible for an ever-increasing number of the world's people, especially those in developed, or industrialized, areas, such as the United States and Europe. Medical researchers constantly make new discoveries about the human body and the many diseases that threaten it. At the same time, doctors and engineers collaborate in creating new medical devices and techniques for diagnosing and treating these diseases.

Among the most ingenious and astonishing of these devices and techniques are those in the fields of *nuclear medicine* and *radiology*. These related disciplines use radiation—various kinds of invisible rays—to view bones, tissue, and organs, even those hidden in the most obscure recesses of a patient's body. Nuclear medicine and radiology allow doctors to find, identify, and treat diseases and other medical problems.

Before Modern Medicine

Up until the early years of the 20th century, before the days of advanced medical radiology and nuclear medicine, the interior of the living human body was largely terra incognita, an unknown territory that doctors and surgeons only partially understood. Even when doctors strongly believed they knew what was wrong with a patient, there was still no way to be certain without actually performing surgery. There was no way to anticipate, before the first incision was made, how complicated a surgical challenge the doctor might face or how to prepare for such a challenge.

To be sure, as medical students, young doctors routinely studied the body's interior. But their experience was limited to dissecting, or cutting up and observing, the limbs and organs of cadavers, or dead bodies. Working only on cadavers was poor preparation for the task of operating on the living bodies of suffering patients. For this reason, before the advent of medical radiology and nuclear medicine, the type of surgery most often performed was the amputation of injured limbs. Little corrective surgery was done on internal organs, and such advanced techniques as open-heart and brain surgery were unknown.

The fields of medical diagnosis and surgery took a giant leap forward with the development of radiology, the first medical discipline to use radiation as a tool. Most of the basic principles of radiology were first observed and developed in the 18th and 19th centuries. Particularly important to this development were discoveries made in three fields—vacuums, electricity, and materials that can record visual images.

Vacuum and Electricity Experiments

The first scientifically recognized vacuum was produced in Florence, Italy, in 1643 by a scientist named Evangelista Torricelli. Several years later, in 1646, Otto von Guericke, a town official of Magdeburg, Germany, created a device that could efficiently remove air from a container to produce an even better vacuum. Von Guericke also worked with the phenomenon of static electricity, creating a machine that generated electric sparks. It is said that von Guericke was the first person to have witnessed human-made electric light.

Von Guericke's work provided the foundation for a succession of researchers over the next two centuries who were interested in the relationship between electricity and glass globes containing vacuums. Finally, in the 19th century, England's Sir William Crookes succeeded in developing glass tubes with previously unmatched high vacuums. When, in the 1860s and 1870s, he put wire terminals, called the cathode and the anode, at opposite ends of a vacuum tube and sent electricity through the cathode, an electric current traveled across the airless gap with relative ease.

During his experiments, Crookes noticed that part of the tube's circular wall glowed mysteriously. He believed that the glow was caused by some kind of invisible rays, which he and other scientists subsequently called cathode rays. Although he was unaware of it at the time, Crookes had actually generated *X rays*, a kind of pure energy having no mass and no electrical charge. The scientist repeatedly found boxes of photographic plates in his laboratory strangely fogged, as though exposed to light. Not connecting the fogged plates with his experiments, he kept complaining to the photographic plate manufacturer and receiving replacements. Finally, the platemaker suggested

The British scientist Sir William Crookes holds one of the vacuum tubes he developed that were eventually used to generate X rays.

that Crookes himself might be doing something in his laboratory that caused the fogging. Confident that he had checked and rechecked his steps, Crookes rejected such a suggestion.

Image Recording

The story of Crookes and his fogged plates illustrates how radiology is related to photography. Like photography, radiology depended on the development of new types of sensitized material for recording the images produced by various kinds of radiation. That is why the beginning of X-ray image recording is very closely tied to advances in photographic image recording.

The first light-sensitive chemical mixture, silver chloride, was discovered in 1727 by a German chemist named Johann H. Schulz. A few years later, a Swedish chemist, Carl Wilhelm Scheele, produced an image of the sun's spectrum, or component colors, on a piece of paper coated with the same light-sensitive mixture. Over the next century, a series of experimenters gradually improved the quality of the light-sensitive mixtures and their control over the development process. In 1826, Joseph-Nicéphore Niepce created the first permanent photograph, a crude picture of his house that required an eight-hour exposure. In 1839, the English physicist William Henry Fox Talbot discovered a way to reduce the average exposure time of photographic plates from more than an hour to half a minute. In a letter to Fox Talbot, Sir John Herschel, another researcher, coined the word "photography." Herschel also first used the words "negative" and "positive" to describe the two types of photographic images.

The New Field of Radiology

Eventually, scientists combined knowledge about electricity, vacuums, and image recording to form a new field called radiology. The important event that sparked this development was the discovery and accurate description of X rays in the late 1890s by Wilhelm Conrad Roentgen. He was born in 1845 in Lennep, a small German town in the Rhine River valley. In 1888 he accepted an appointment to the faculty of the physics department of the University of Würzburg. Roentgen set up a small laboratory and involved himself in experiments that personally interested him. He was particularly fascinated with the cathode ray studies of William Crookes.

Late on the afternoon of Friday, November 8, 1895, Roentgen was in his darkened laboratory conducting an experiment that involved passing a high-voltage charge through a Hittorf-Crookes tube, an improved version of the cathode-ray tube. The tube was completely enclosed in a lightproof box. Suddenly, in the darkness, Roentgen noticed a green glow coming from a nearby laboratory tabletop. Lighting a match, Roentgen saw that the source of the glow was a cardboard screen coated with barium platinocyanide, a fluorescent, or glowing, material.

He repeated the experiment, moving the coated screen progressively farther away from the box. The glow continued. Roentgen realized that the glow must result from some kind of invisible rays being emitted by the Crookes tube. Perhaps these were cathode rays, the phenomenon Crookes and others had earlier described. Roentgen observed the rays carefully. He reasoned that if they could penetrate the lightproof box,

Wilhelm Conrad Roentgen, the discoverer of X rays.

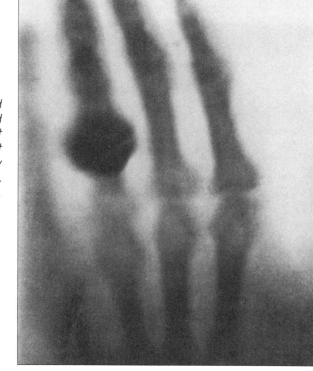

Roentgen discovered that X rays could penetrate certain soft tissues of the body but were blocked by denser substances, such as human bone. This is his first X-ray photograph.

they might be able to go through other materials, too. When Roentgen tried blocking the rays with an assortment of materials, he found that, with the exceptions of lead and platinum, the rays penetrated with ease. For one of his experiments he had his wife, Bertha, place her hand on a photographic plate, and then he directed X rays at her hand for about 15 minutes. When the plate was developed, it showed a skeletal picture of Bertha's hand, complete with the two rings on her fingers!

Highly excited by this strange discovery, Roentgen moved his bed into the laboratory and secluded himself there. He even had his meals delivered outside the door. Roentgen was determined to tell no one of his findings until he completed an exhaustive series of experiments. For seven weeks he experimented in an effort to identify and quantify, or measure, the invisible rays. The scientist also further tested their ability to penetrate all sorts of materials. When the experiments showed that the rays could indeed do what he had first believed they could, that is, penetrate almost any substance, he knew he had discovered a scientific phenomenon unlike any previously known. At the time, Roentgen did not understand the nature of these invisible emanations, so he gave them the name "X rays," because in mathematics "X" stands for an unknown value.

A Momentous Announcement

After many additional tests, Roentgen recorded his findings in an article titled "On a New Kind of Ray, a Preliminary Communication," and submitted it for publication in the journal of the University of Würzburg's Physical Medical Society on December 28, 1895. The article was only 10 pages long but was packed with information.

Roentgen reviewed, in careful detail, each of the steps that had led to the discovery of the strange rays and the many experiments he had performed afterward in order to confirm that X rays were different from any rays previously known. He reported that the penetrating ability of X rays was inversely proportional to the density of the target material exposed to them. In other words, the denser the material, the less X rays were able to penetrate it. Roentgen wrote:

> Paper is very transparent [to the X rays]; I observed that the fluorescent screen still glowed brightly behind a bound book of about 1,000 pages; the printer's ink had no noticeable effect. Likewise, fluorescence appeared behind a double pack of [playing] cards; the eye can hardly detect a single card held between the apparatus and the screen.

The medical community quickly realized that the newly discovered rays had potential value as a diagnostic tool. By passing the rays through a person's body and onto a photographic plate, doctors could literally see inside the body. They could not only observe bones and other internal features without resorting to surgery but also detect, identify, and study various internal problems and abnormalities. Doctors everywhere began using Roentgen's X rays almost immediately in clinical practice, and soon he was famous around the world. In 1901 he became the first person to be awarded the Nobel Prize in physics, and the Physical Society of Stockholm named him an honored member the following year.

The news of Roentgen's dramatic experiments with X rays caused many other researchers to shift their attention to cathode-ray-tube

An early X-ray machine.

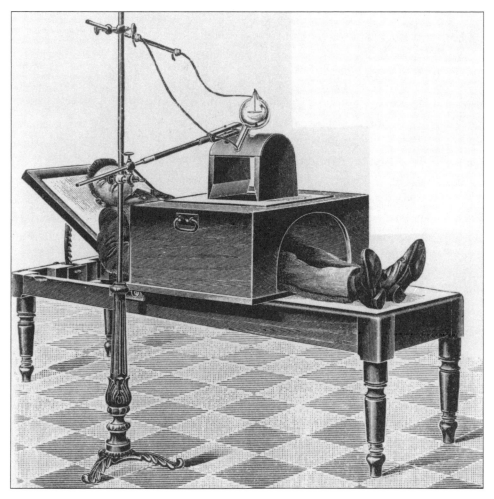

emissions. In the United States, Professor Michael Pupin at Columbia University in New York City produced an image using X rays on January 2, 1896, approximately two weeks after Roentgen made his initial announcement. Also in the United States, the renowned inventor Thomas Alva Edison began to experiment with X rays not long after the news of Roentgen's discovery became public. Edison's particular interest was in *fluoroscopy*, which is the viewing of X-ray images on a screen at the moment they are being made. Edison discovered a useful improvement in the photosensitive coating used for image reproduction, but he ceased experimentation when one of his laboratory assistants suffered severe X-ray burns.

X Rays Grow in Medical Importance

Just two years after its discovery, the X-ray process, or "roentgenology," as it was then called in honor of Roentgen, was put to use saving lives on a large scale by the U.S. Army during the Spanish-American War in Cuba. Army surgeons aboard the hospital ship *Relief* used X-ray devices to locate and safely remove bullets and shell fragments from inside the bodies of wounded soldiers. A number of these same surgeons had served earlier in the Civil War, and they recalled how many lives and limbs were lost then for the lack of such a miraculous machine. On the home front, many American surgeons began using X-ray devices to locate foreign objects in patients' bodies and to study serious fractures before they performed surgical procedures.

Probably because X rays were considered to be so exotic, the general public was intensely interested in them. Before long, so-called roentgenologists opened for business in offices and storefronts all over the United States. Many of these people had no medical training. Instead, they presented shiny, button-covered X-ray machines as their main attractions, and X rays quickly became a fad. Having a bony X ray taken of a hand or a foot became a popular pastime and diversion for large numbers of curious and fascinated people across the country. The new fad became the subject of much humor. One of many comical commentaries is the following poem that appeared in an 1896 edition of the journal *Photography*:

The Roentgen Rays, the Roentgen Rays,
What is this craze:
The town's ablaze
With the new phase
Of x-ray's ways.
I'm full of daze,
Shock and amaze,
For now-a-days
I hear they'll gaze
Thro' cloak and gown, and even stays,
These naughty, naughty Roentgen Rays.

While at first the main use for X rays was seeing inside the body, some researchers were interested in the potential of X rays to treat diseases. Doctors soon began experimenting with the rays in efforts to kill cultures, or colonies grown in the laboratory, of such deadly diseases as tuberculosis, typhus, cholera, and diphtheria. In these investigations, the experimenters attempted to use X rays to cure various types of cancer. In 1896, the *Chicago Times* reported that a doctor had exposed two patients with cancer of the stomach to one hour of X rays, with beneficial results. That same year, a French physician, Dr. V. Despeignes, reported in the French medical publication *Lyon Medicale* that the application of X rays in two cases, one of cancer of the stomach and the other of the mouth, "had a distinct anesthetic [pain-reducing] effect and caused a general improvement in the condition of the patient, but exerted little influence upon the growth."

But despite these promising reports, most doctors claimed disappointing results from such experiments. The main reason for this lack of success was that the early X-ray equipment was quite primitive by today's standards. Many manufacturers with little or no understanding of X rays rushed machines into production to meet the growing demand and turned out crudely designed equipment. Some were so dangerous that the X-ray tubes periodically exploded and the celluloid-based photographic plates then in use sometimes caught fire.

Another danger, even with those machines that were well crafted, was that they provided little control over radiation output or a means of measuring the dosages they emitted. At the time, users were unaware that the rays had the potential for damaging living cells and tissue. Because of this ignorance, many early X-ray machine operators innocently inflicted serious burns on themselves and their patients. Soon, a number of researchers began commenting on the potential of the new rays to burn the skin. One of the most eloquent of these warnings came from the renowned Scottish doctor Sir Joseph Lister, who stated in September 1896:

> There is another way in which the Roentgen rays connect themselves with physiology [living bodies] and may possibly influence medicine. It is found that if the skin is long exposed to their actions it becomes very much irritated, affected with a sort of aggravated sunburning. This suggests the idea that the transmission of the rays through the human body may be not altogether a matter of indifference to [having no effect upon] internal organs but may by long continued action produce, according to the condition of the part concerned, injurous irritation or . . . stimulation.

But most X-ray users believed that the sunburnlike effects of the rays were relatively harmless and that no other significant dangers existed. They had no idea that large doses could cause cancer, and, tragically, many doctors and operators eventually contracted the disease because of their long-term exposure to the rays.

Improvements in Speed and Quality

Soon after Roentgen discovered X rays in 1895, he and other early radiologists realized that they needed a new type of sensitive material to receive X-ray images, one that was specially made for the purpose. The ordinary photographic plates then available were formulated for use in conventional photography using visible light and were only slightly sensitive to invisible X rays. As a result, those who practiced radiology had to make educated guesses about exposure and development times. The production of useful X-ray images then was far more an art than a science.

But researchers soon made many important advances in X-ray machines and their related technology. The highly flammable photographic film was soon replaced by glass plates made specifically for X rays. To improve contrast in the images of the body's various internal parts, researchers devised contrast media, materials that when swallowed made a patient's internal systems show up more clearly. In 1897, Boston researcher Walter Cannon performed experiments that led to the use of the chemical compound barium sulfate as a contrast medium for outlining the digestive tract. And, following Edison's lead, a special type of X-ray machine, the fluoroscope, was developed. This device permitted doctors to see the body's internal parts in action and was therefore a sort of X-ray motion picture.

Since that time, researchers and manufacturers have worked hard to improve the quality and reliability of image materials, chemicals, and other equipment used in radiology. Scientists and doctors recognized the need to control precisely the dosage of X-ray emissions. Initially this was to protect patients and medical personnel from the rays' more extreme dangers, especially cancer. Later, doctors realized that accurate control of dosage was crucial to the proper therapeutic, or curative, application of X rays to skin lesions, or abnormal growths, and underlying cancers. However, it was 40 years before a standardized system of unit dosage for X rays was established at a 1937 international conference. Until then, doctors and technicians had arrived at dosages by a combination of experience and guesswork.

Further Research in Radiation

While researchers worked to expand the use of X rays, experimenters were busy trying to learn more about other types of radiation. It is now known that X rays are related to both radio waves and ordinary light waves and that they are all examples of a phenomenon called electromagnetic radiation. Scientists found that some other kinds of radiation could be used for medical purposes besides X-ray diagnosis. In 1896, French scientist Henri Becquerel began investigating something Roentgen had discovered, that certain rocks fluoresced, or glowed, when exposed to X rays and that some of these rocks continued glowing

Henri Becquerel in his laboratory. Becquerel experimented with uranium ore and discovered that it gave off a mysterious radiation similar to X rays.

long after being exposed. A few years earlier, Becquerel had found that when pitchblende, a brownish black ore containing the element uranium, was exposed to ultraviolet light, it glowed. While preparing to expose the material to X rays, Becquerel discovered by accident that it gave off an invisible radiation even without such exposure. Although Becquerel suspected that uranium was the source of the rays, he could not prove it at the time.

The French husband-and-wife research team of Pierre and Marie Curie continued and improved upon Becquerel's work. In the late 1890s, the Curies were studying the radioactive element radium. When Pierre noticed that the emissions from radium killed diseased cells in the blood of laboratory animals, he realized that the rays had medical potential. Marie Curie later demonstrated that the rays were not X rays but a wholly different kind of radiation. She gave the phenomenon of invisible radiation from the *atoms* of certain elements the name *radioactivity*. In 1903, the Curies jointly received the Nobel Prize for physics, and in 1911, Marie Curie, by now a widow, received another Nobel Prize in chemistry for her work with radium and its compounds. Her research was interrupted by the beginning of World War I in 1914.

Marie Curie, the discoverer of radium.

So Marie Curie turned her attention to the manufacture of X-ray equipment for the Allied armies and to the training of French and American soldiers as roentgenologists.

By the turn of the century, many scientists wondered about the nature of the rays emitted by radium, uranium, and other radioactive substances. Such questions went unanswered until 1903, when British scientist Ernest Rutherford discovered two types of radiation, which he named *alpha* and *beta particles*. Later, a far more powerful emission from uranium was discovered and named gamma radiation. Rutherford's subsequent experiments with radiation eventually led him to conceive of the 20th century's first widely accepted description of the atom and its structure. According to this view, the atom consists of a central nucleus made up of smaller particles called protons and neutrons. Revolving around the nucleus, like planets around the sun, are energetic particles called *electrons*. One significant aspect of this discovery for all scientists was the idea that all atoms are divisible into smaller parts, and that these parts—the protons, neutrons, electrons, and other particles—can, under certain conditions, be emitted, or given off, by atoms. The concept of atoms giving off highly energetic particles was the most important aspect of the atomic theory, from a medical point of view. Doctors and medical researchers realized that these showers of atomic particles constituted the mysterious invisible rays that showed so much promise in medical diagnosis and treatment.

The theoretical work done by scientists such as Rutherford set the basis for much of the medical research that came next. The treatment of deep-lying cancers was undertaken using two types of radioactive implants. One was a permanent implant that most often consisted of radioactive thin gold seeds about one-fifth of an inch in length. The radiation emitted by the seeds helped to destroy many of the cancer cells. By the end of three weeks these seeds lost 99% of their radiant energy. Other temporary implants were needles made of platinum, or sometimes steel, that contained radium.

Meanwhile, the theoretical scientists continued their valuable work. In 1923, Hungarian chemist Georg Karl von Hevesy was the first person to suggest a medical use for radioisotopes. These are radioac-

The interior of a hospital X-ray department around 1919.

tively unstable versions of many normal elements. Hevesy's idea was to inject these subtances into plants and animals and then to trace their movements using radioactively sensitive instruments. The substances became known also as *radionuclides*, or tracers. This notion was to have major implications for nuclear medicine as a diagnostic tool.

By this time, medical science was actively pursuing the two main and distinct courses in the use of radiation and radioactive substances: diagnosis and treatment. Researchers were enthusiastically finding or creating many new versions of these substances for medical use. By 1936, 18 radioisotopes of medical significance were being manufactured at the Lawrence cyclotron in Livermore, California. Ten years later, in 1946, 20 different medically useful radioisotopes were being produced at the government's Oak Ridge, Tennessee, atomic energy plant. In the same decade, radioactive iodine was first used in the diagnosis and treatment of thyroid disorders. This marked the true beginning of nuclear medicine's role as a regular clinical diagnostic tool.

CHAPTER 2

THE USE OF RADIONUCLIDES

This cyclotron at the Argonne National Laboratory is used to bombard substances with atomic particles, turning them into radioactive isotopes with medical applications.

Radionuclides are also known variously as radioisotopes, markers, or tracers, depending on how they are to be used. Although some radioactive materials do occur naturally in nature—radium, for example—the majority of medical radionuclides are made artificially, in atomic reactors. Medical versions of these reactors are often small and very expensive devices called cyclotrons, owned and operated in-house by large hospitals.

Radionuclides work by giving off a type of radiation known as *gamma rays*. Similar in many ways to X rays, gamma rays have no mass. An important difference between the two kinds of radiation is that gamma rays are given off by natural and artificial radioactive materials, whereas in most cases X rays are generated by a machine. In the body, different radionuclide compounds are absorbed in greater concentrations by different types of tissue, which means that certain organs can be targeted for study by using specific radionuclides. To the extent that they help make organs and tissue more visible, radionuclides function much like the contrast media used in making X-ray exposures, except, of course, that radionuclides contain radioactive materials and X-ray contrast media do not.

The reason that radioisotopes work so well as tracers in the body is that these radioactive versions of common elements are absorbed by various bodily organs and tissues in exactly the same manner as the nonradioactive versions. This is because both radioactive and nonradioactive versions of the elements are chemically the same. As Dr. Joseph Sacks, formerly of Northwestern University and an authority on radioactive isotopes, puts it:

> The fundamental property that makes it possible to use isotopes as tracers is that all the isotopes of an element have identical chemical properties. This applies whether the isotopes are the naturally occurring stable ones or the radioactive ones that are produced by nuclear reactors. The distinctive physical property which serves to detect and measure the concentration of the isotope in question is independent of the chemical transformations that the element may undergo [in becoming radioactive]. The chemical properties of the element are determined entirely by the number and configuration [placement around the atomic nucleus] of the extranuclear, or planetary, electrons. These are identical for all the isotopes of any given element.

Ernest R. Rutherford, who developed an early theory of the internal structure of the atom and discovered that alpha particles, high-speed protons, could be used in a way similar to X rays.

Radionuclides have proven to be of great value for many scientific purposes. Before these artificial substances could become practical for medical use, a way had to be found to produce them in relatively large quantities at reasonable prices. The radionuclides also had to be reasonably stable and therefore predictable in their results.

A major step toward the development of radionuclides was accomplished by Ernest Rutherford in 1919 at the Cavendish Laboratory in Cambridge, England. Working with radium, Rutherford discovered an energy wave of particles that, like X rays, could penetrate solid mate-

John H. Lawrence, who invented the cyclotron, which produces radioactive materials for use as tracer elements.

rials and produce an image on a photographic plate. This strange energy, Rutherford showed, consisted of positively charged nuclear protons, or alpha particles. Radium was, however, a poor source of alpha particles. A far more powerful source had to be discovered before significant progress could be made.

A breakthrough in the creation of such a source was achieved in 1931 at the University of California's Radiation Laboratory by physicist Ernest O. Lawrence. Lawrence invented the cyclotron, which used a large and powerful magnetic field to accelerate atomic particles to very high velocities. This process succeeded in producing radioactive elements with a radiation power equal to huge quantities of radium. However, the costs involved in the process still kept medically useful radioactive materials too expensive for ordinary clinical or hospital use. The construction of an atomic reactor by the United States government at Oak Ridge, Tennessee, during World War II solved many of these problems. When the reactor was made available for civilian use after the war, there finally was a way to produce a wide range of radioisotopes in large quantities at a much lower cost.

The First Nuclear Patients

Another important experimental use of radioactive materials for medical treatment began in the mid-1930s when American medical researcher Dr. John H. Lawrence of the University of California at Berkeley undertook an investigation of the therapeutic possibilities of radioactive phosphorous. Lawrence decided to administer the radioactive isotope phosphorous 32 to rats suffering from leukemia, a type of cancer, as well as from lymphoma, the development of tumors in the body's lymph system. To his astonishment, the diseases disappeared and the mice recovered. Apparently, the radiation had eliminated the diseased cells by damaging or destroying the cells' reproductive abilities. At the same time, nearly all of the normal, healthy cells remained undamaged. Thus, the radiation had selectively killed the dangerous cells.

After additional studies confirmed these results, the first human patient, a person diagnosed as suffering from chronic leukemia, was treated with radioactive phosphorous 32 on December 24, 1936, at the Radiation Laboratory at Berkeley. The immediate results were so promising that soon several more leukemia patients began the same treatment. In a subsequent and even more promising development, Lawrence's first patient was still alive and free of disease some 20 years later. Another radionuclide, radioactive iodine, was used by doctors in the late 1930s and early 1940s to treat thyroid cancer.

When World War II ended, in 1945, many members of the general public began to show increasing hostility toward the use of radioactive materials in all fields, including medicine. These feelings resulted from fear about the devastating effects of the atomic bombs the United States dropped on Japan. Many people mistakenly equated the type of atomic energy used in these weapons with the kind used for medical diagnosis and treatment. Whereas an atomic bomb releases a large, uncontrolled amount of radiation that can maim and kill, the atomic substances used by doctors release very small amounts of radiation in a highly controlled manner. The results are beneficial rather than harmful. Because of public misconceptions about atomic energy, in the late 1940s and early 1950s people working in the atomic industry began vigorously promoting therapeutic and lifesaving uses for radioactive materials.

Radioactive Implants

One such therapeutic use of radioactive substances is in radioactive implants. Contained within tiny capsules, these radioactive materials are placed inside of a patient's body, where they shrink or destroy certain types of tumors using a localized high dose of radiation. This treatment is most often called for in the treatment of cancers of the uterus, vagina, cervix, and rectum. In such cases, it is possible to insert and remove the capsule without surgery.

Several different radionuclides are now commonly used for radioactive implants. One is an isotope of arsenic. Although arsenic is deadly to humans when taken in sufficient quantities, a much smaller and safer amount of this radioactive material can be used to detect the presence of a brain tumor.

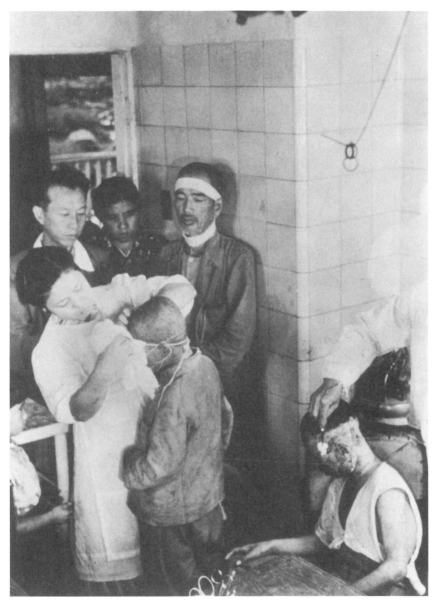

This photograph, taken in August 1945, shows victims of the Hiroshima atomic bomb blast awaiting treatment for radiation burns. The effects of the atomic bomb made the American public wary of radiation therapy.

Another common tracer is the element cesium. In a nonsurgical procedure, one or more tiny capsules containing radioactive cesium are placed inside the body near the site of a tumor. The capsules are left in place for a period of time determined by a radiologist, and they deliver gamma radiation to the cancer. While the capsules are in place, the patient must remain in the hospital. The patient's bed may be surrounded by a lead fence in order to protect others from the radiation. All materials associated with the treatment, including the patient's body wastes, must be disposed of by carefully planned and monitored means. The duration of treatment can range from hours up to several days, after which the capsules are removed and the patient can go home, usually experiencing little or no aftereffects.

Radioactive iodine is a radionuclide that has been used since the early 1940s to treat hyperthyroidism, a condition in which the thyroid gland is overly active, releasing greater than normal amounts of thyroid hormones. This results in such symptoms as a speed-up of the body's metabolism, or chemical processes, as well as nervousness, rapid heartbeat, weight loss, fatigue, and excessive sweating. Before the advent of nuclear medicine, this serious condition had to be treated by surgically removing part of the thyroid gland. Radioactive iodine is used today to treat about 20,000 Americans yearly, replacing surgery as the most common treatment of hyperthyroidism. The number of patients who undergo surgery for thyroid gland problems each year has fallen from a high of 3,000 to fewer than 50. The radioactive iodine works by being absorbed into the thyroid tissue and then destroying diseased cells. The doctor or technician carefully regulates the dosage so that, in most cases, enough undamaged tissue is left for the patient to maintain normal functioning of the thyroid.

Another tracer, radioactive gallium, can detect the presence of pneumonia in the body well before it is detectable by conventional X rays. The radioactive gallium is injected and the patient waits one to two days for it to circulate fully throughout the body and build up at the site of the problem. Because the doctor frequently does not know where the pneumonia is lodged, most of the patient's body will be scanned and imaged.

This machine detects concentrations of iodine radioisotopes that reveal problems with the thyroid gland.

Still another useful radionuclide, radioactive indium, is particularly effective at locating areas of internal infection, a condition that can follow surgery. Because radioactive indium works in cooperation with the body's own white blood cells, it must first be joined with these cells. This is accomplished by taking a small amount of blood from the patient and mixing it with the radioactive material in the laboratory. Then the mixture is reinjected into the patient's body, where it is effective in seeking out and marking areas of infection. Scanning with detection instruments can begin just a few hours after injection.

Experiments aimed at finding new ways to use radionuclides are conducted every year in labs around the world. These versatile substances will, no doubt, continue to be one of the medical community's most useful tools for both diagnosing and treating several harmful diseases.

CHAPTER 3

NUCLEAR DIAGNOSTICS

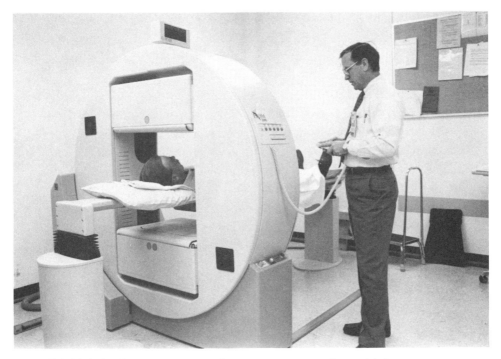

This high-tech camera records gamma rays and very high energy radiation and can produce a scan of the entire human body.

Nuclear medicine is used in a number of ways to diagnose illness. One way is illustrated in the following hypothetical but quite common situation. A nuclear medical technologist who is also a doctor finishes his daily equipment check just as the first patient of the day, a young boy, arrives. The child is cheerful and active but looks unusually thin. He has lost weight quite suddenly, and his doctor suspects that the problem might be an overly active thyroid. Fortunately for the boy, nuclear medical technologists have more experience in diagnosing this particular condition than any other. The day before, the technician had given the boy a taste-free "atomic cocktail" of radioactive iodine to drink, after which the iodine had 24 hours to concentrate itself in the thyroid gland. The technician helps the youngster up onto the gamma ray camera table and then takes a scan of the boy's thyroid gland. The developed picture does indeed show a thyroid problem, so the child is instructed to return soon to the same lab for nuclear medicine treatment to correct it.

An estimated 120 million nuclear medicine procedures are performed yearly in the United States. Probably the most common of these procedures is nuclear scanning, the one just described. The primary function of nuclear scanning, also known as radionuclide organ imaging, or scintigraphy, is to aid doctors in measuring organ function and in diagnosing and treating disease. This technology—which includes various scintillation, or nuclear detection and scanning, devices— makes it possible to outline the size, shape, and exact location of an organ, or even of a very small chamber or duct within that organ.

Nuclear Detection Devices

The first nuclear scanning device was the scintillation scanner, or dot scanner, developed in 1949 by Dr. Benedict Cassen at the University of California, Los Angeles. As Dr. John H. Lawrence explained in his book *Radioisotopes and Radiation*, in the dot scanner

> A . . . scintillation counter detected the radiation, and the counts were then recorded by means of a tapper bar making corresponding points [black ink dots] on a piece of paper. The number of dots recorded in a given area was proportional to the amount of activity detected. The early dot scanner did not contain any means for screening out low-energy scattered, or background, radiation [which occurs naturally everywhere on earth]. It was successful for the thyroid scanning

because the thyroid gland lies just beneath the skin surface so that scanning is minimal. Before scanning techniques could be applied successfully to organs which lie deeper, improvements in instrumentation [more efficient machine parts and design] to deal with this problem of scatter were needed.

Cassen and others made these improvements, and the dot scanner became popular with medical technicians, especially because it was

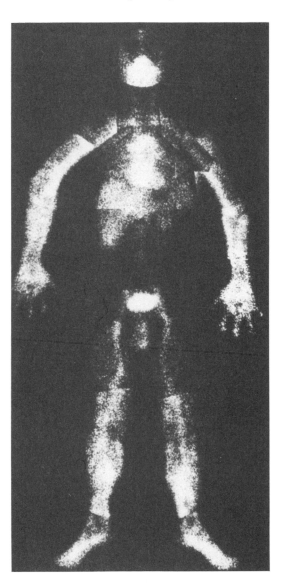

This composite photograph shows the movement of radioactive isotopes through the human body.

able to show the distribution of radioactive iodine within a patient's thyroid gland. The device was moved by hand over a patient's thyroid, a tiring process for technician and patient as it required several hours to achieve a reading. Cassen later devised a mechanism that moved the scanner automatically. This more advanced machine, known as a rectilinear scanner, is still in use today.

A patient at Cumberland Memorial Hospital in Cumberland, Maryland, receives a nuclear medical scan.

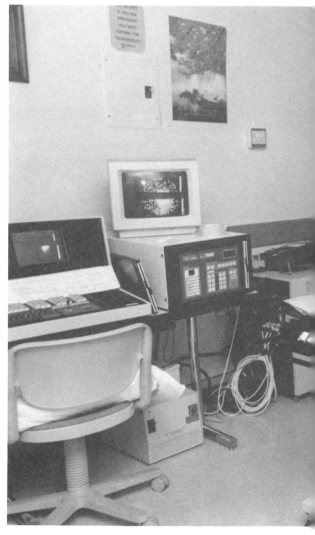

During most of the 1960s, physicians' diagnostic needs continued to be served primarily by Cassen's rectilinear camera and a growing number of radionuclides. The camera was quite primitive by today's standards. However, the major problem was the danger to patients of the high levels of radioactivity found in the radionuclides then in use. This limited the quantity of materials that could be safely administered

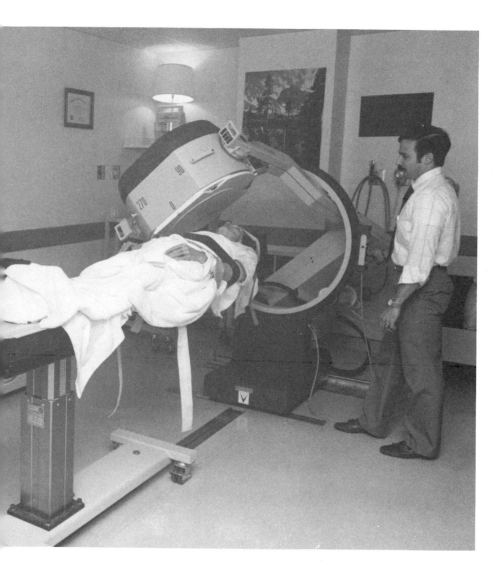

and correspondingly increased the amount of time required to complete a single scan.

In 1958, Dr. Hal Anger announced the invention of the scintillation camera, a different type of scanner that he had been working on for four years. However, the scintillation camera did not become clinically useful right away, because it did not perform well with the low-energy radionuclides then available. With the introduction in the late 1960s and 1970s of a powerful synthetic radionuclide, technetium 99, the scintillation camera finally came into popular use.

In 1965 Anger introduced the tomographic scanner. The word "tomography" comes from the Greek word for slice; in effect, these devices allow doctors to use radiation to slice through the body's outer tissue and reveal what lies beneath. The tomographic scanner was the first device capable of giving multiple images at predetermined planes, or depths, from a single scan of a patient. In other words, the machine produced a crude three-dimensional image. Although this early version of the tomographic scanner rendered unacceptable images for clinical use, it later evolved into the successful system now known as computer tomography.

Nuclear medicine first began experiencing rapid growth in the decade of the 1960s, due largely to the introduction of the tracer material technetium 99. Technetium 99 found particular use in brain scans, to detect and locate tumors. A significant development was the introduction of a system whereby technetium 99 could be made right in the hospital. This led to a double breakthrough: by producing technetium 99 on-site, hospitals could make the radioisotope available around the clock to patients; and because the material lost its radioactivity quickly inside the patient's body, it could be administered safely in stronger doses. The results were shorter, faster exposures and better images, especially when used in combination with the improved scintillation camera.

With its many winning advantages, nuclear diagnostic medicine finally began to come into its own. The number of nuclear scans done in American hospitals each year climbed into the millions as the procedures' uses and flexibility increased. In 1971, the American

Medical Association recognized the importance of the field of nuclear medicine by declaring it to be a separate and distinct medical specialty.

Today's Nuclear Imaging Equipment

The next great advance in nuclear diagnostic devices came in the late 1970s, when researchers combined scanning equipment with computers to produce much more powerful diagnostic systems. Put simply, a computer's superior ability to read, interpret, and store information greatly increased the amount of diagnostic information that could be produced with each diagnostic test.

Improvements in imaging instruments and in methods for evaluating data have produced notable advances in the nuclear medicine field. Unlike X-ray equipment, which gives off radioactive waves that pass through the patient's body to create an image on X-ray film, modern nuclear medicine technology provides wholly new ways to deliver radioactive rays for viewing the body's interior. Today, doctors can choose from three basic kinds of devices for nuclear imaging: gamma ray camera, the SPECT scanner, and the PET scanner.

The gamma ray camera combines radionuclide and computer technology. When a radionuclide has been delivered inside a patient's body, the gamma ray emissions from it can be detected by the gamma ray camera. Gamma rays given off by the radionuclide strike receptors in the camera and generate electronic signals, which are sent to a computer that converts them into a picture. Although the gamma ray camera does not create as highly detailed a picture of the body's interior as other imaging devices can, it is very good at recording concentrations of radionuclides in tissue and organs. By noting how much radionuclide an organ has absorbed, a doctor can decide whether the organ is overactive, underactive, or normal. Knowing this can significantly affect the patient's course of treatment, because a number of diseases will cause changes in activity levels within organs long before they produce the physical changes that X rays can show. Specific examples of radionuclide scanning's advantages are its ability to detect tiny areas

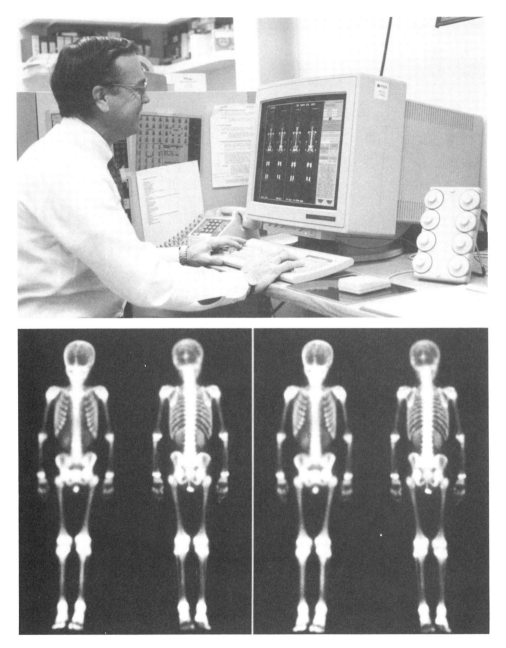

This computer monitor enhances the image produced by a scan of the human skeletal system and allows the doctor to manipulate the image to gain more knowledge of a patient's condition.

of tissue damage caused by a heart attack and to spot cancerous tumors in their early stages. Such early detection makes earlier treatment possible, which usually increases a patient's chances for recovery.

The second kind of nuclear imaging device is the SPECT scanner. SPECT stands for *single photon emission computer tomography*. The SPECT scanner is, in effect, a ring of gamma cameras that rotate around the patient. The SPECT takes many closely spaced pictures of the interior of the patient's body in a series of "slices." These pictures are then put together by a computer to create an amazingly realistic three-dimensional image. It is particularly useful with heart attacks in showing how much muscle damage has been suffered and how much pumping effectiveness the heart has lost.

The PET scanner is considered by doctors to be the present state-of-the-art, or most technically advanced, nuclear imaging device. The name "PET" stands for *positron emission tomography*. PET scanners are more efficient in radionuclide detection than SPECT scanners. The device has become a valuable addition to the collection of diagnostic tools available to doctors, because PET allows them to view chemical and biological processes of the body, and particularly of the brain, in motion pictures. A patient lies on a table with his or her head in a ring of gamma ray detectors, and a radionuclide version of a substance found normally in the brain—glucose, for example—is delivered to the patient's brain.

As the radionuclide particles in the brain release their rays of tiny atomic particles, called positrons, the revolving ring of detectors picks up the emissions. When converted by a computer into a motion picture, the result is a movie showing the metabolic processes of the patient's brain.

A limitation of the PET scanner at present is the fact that the positron-emitting material it uses has a very short radioactive life. In other words, the substance rapidly loses its radioactive qualities. Because it must be used and replenished quickly, it must be manufactured on-site in a small cyclotron by skilled technicians. This makes the PET scanner a very expensive imaging device to own and operate, and presently it is installed in only a few, large medical centers. It is expected that PET scanners will eventually become more widely available, for they are unmatched in delivering images of otherwise undetectable brain disorders—tiny blood vessel blockages and tumors—as well as in revealing chemical signs of brain dysfunctions leading to mental conditions, such as manic depression, schizophrenia, epilepsy, and Alzheimer's disease. Doctors hope that in time PET technology will become useful for studying the metabolism of other organs, too.

Scanning Procedures, Step by Step

From a patient's viewpoint, preparing for a scan by a nuclear imaging device is simple and relatively painless. The procedure for a gamma ray camera scan is typical. After drinking a liquid containing a radionuclide material or receiving an injection, the patient must wait long enough for the material to move through the body. When a significant amount of the radionuclide has been absorbed by the organ that is to be examined, the patient is asked to lie or sit down, depending on the type of picture to be taken. The gamma camera is positioned close to the patient's body; then it takes a series of pictures as the radionuclide material travels along in the bloodstream. The result is a virtual "motion picture" of such functions as blood flow and the body's gastrointestinal activities. The patient will experience no discomfort during this process. There may be a brief chilly sensation when the material is first injected.

The patient undergoing a scan may receive one of two general types of diagnosis—in vivo or in vitro. The phrase "in vivo" translates as "in life," and it refers to diagnostic testing done directly within the patient's body. The other term, "in vitro," which translates literally as "in a glass vessel," simply means any process carried out in a laboratory to test fluids or materials that have been taken from a patient's body for this purpose. In nuclear medicine, both of these techniques are valuable for finding out what a patient's problem may be. For some patients, especially when a serious condition is involved, both types of testing may be performed.

But before a doctor calls for any type of test, an important first step is to review a detailed medical history of the patient. By knowing the patient's previous medical experiences and listening to a description of the current symptoms, the doctor can often narrow the list down to just a few possibilities. At that point, testing can be done to pinpoint the problem.

Doctors have many specific nuclear medicine tests to pick from, depending on their patients' particular problems. One of these tests is the lung scan, used to detect blood clots and other abnormalities in the lungs. The patient is given an injection of radioactive albumin particles. Albumin is a protein found in almost all tissue. When the radioactive albumin reaches the lungs in sufficient quantity, usually in about an hour, gamma camera pictures are taken to show the dispersion, or spreading out, of the albumin particles and to reveal any unusual distribution patterns. Along with this scan, the doctor frequently will order a standard lung X ray and possibly other tests before and after the albumin scan, to obtain additional information.

Another nuclear medicine test, the brain scan, is used to investigate possible brain illnesses, such as infection, stroke, tumor, and blood supply problems. First, the patient is given an injection of a radioactive material. Then a gamma camera takes pictures of the head: from the front, back, each side, and sometimes the top. When testing brain-blood circulation, many pictures will be taken shortly after the injection; more pictures will be taken later to see how much of the radioactive material still remains in the brain.

The "thyroid uptake and scan" is used to diagnose disorders of the thyroid gland. Depending on the doctor's decision, the patient will receive radioactive iodine either by mouth or by injection. When taken by mouth, the test is performed the following day, in order to allow the iodine to circulate throughout the body. When injected, the iodine circulates very rapidly, so that the test can be performed after only about 20 minutes. The test can then be done either by an in vivo, or scanning, procedure, or by an in vitro procedure involving a laboratory blood test. In the first case, a gamma ray camera scan will show how actively the thyroid is working and whether any portions of the gland are underactive or inactive. In the second, a blood test shows how much fluid secreted by the thyroid is circulating in the bloodstream.

Cardiac imaging, another common nuclear medicine test, is used to study advanced coronary artery disease, to detect a recent heart

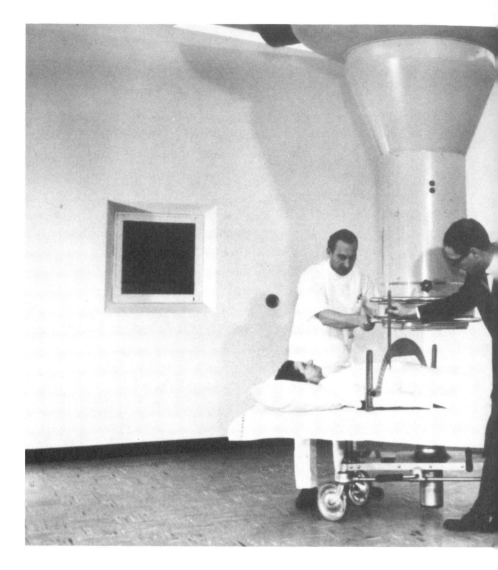

attack, or to discover the beginning of heart problems when they are otherwise undetectable. For a heart blood-flow evaluation, a radioactive material is injected into the patient's body, usually while he or she exercises, and a gamma ray camera scan is taken immediately. After three to four hours, another exposure is taken and the two pictures are

This large X-ray machine was considered state-of-the-art during the 1950s.

compared. To check on heart function, the doctor takes pictures of the heart after radioactive material is injected and then a computer analysis tells how efficiently the heart is operating. To identify a recent heart attack, the gamma ray camera takes a scan two to four hours following the injection of radioactive material.

In liver and gallbladder imaging, nuclear scanning techniques can diagnose liver disorders, such as cirrhosis or tumors, and also gallbladder disease. To study the liver, a gamma ray camera scan is taken of the organ 15 minutes after the injection of a radioactive material. The distribution pattern of the material tells how well the liver is functioning. For a test of the gallbladder, scans of the organ are made within an hour or more of a radioactive material injection; follow-ups are often done within the next four hours. The test can reveal gallbladder disease and also yield additional information about the liver.

Still another nuclear medicine test, the bone scan, is used to measure bone growth and bone density and to detect bone fractures, tumors, and bone infections. A special radioactive material that finds its way to the bones is injected. Two to three hours later, a gamma ray camera picture is taken. This is usually a full-body scan. The doctor may order conventional X rays as well, in order to help confirm the diagnosis.

In addition to these and other imaging tests, doctors have other nuclear medicine tools to work with. Some of these are nonimaging tests. In these procedures, the doctor or technician gives a radioactive compound to the patient either orally or by injection. Afterward, samples of the patient's tissue or blood or other fluids are taken and tested in vitro. When studied in the laboratory, these samples often tell doctors many things about the condition of the particular organ or body system being tested. This is just one more way that nuclear medicine helps millions of people around the world obtain a clear and accurate diagnosis and thereby ensure that the treatment they receive is proper and effective.

CHAPTER 4

A VARIETY OF RADIATION THERAPIES

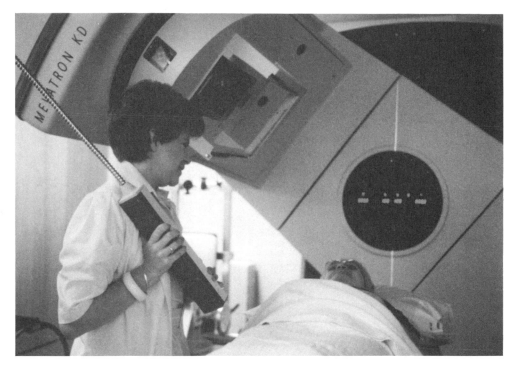

This linear accelerator at the Guthrie Medical Center in Sayre, Pennsylvania, generates high-speed subatomic particles that can kill diseased cells and shrink tumors.

The following situation, routine in modern hospitals, shows how a typical radiation therapy procedure works. A radiology technologist in the midst of her average busy day sees that the next patient on her schedule is a woman who has had a mastectomy, or the removal of a breast in which a cancerous tumor had developed. The patient's doctor has prescribed X-ray radiation therapy to kill any cancer cells that may remain in the affected area. The technologist, seeing that the woman is depressed and scared, tells her about the many mastectomy patients who have been treated at the hospital and are now fully restored to health and enjoying normal lives. The patient listens to the technologist with interest and cheers up somewhat.

The technologist then works intensively with the radiologist, a physician, to figure out a precise dosage, exposure site, and treatment schedule for the patient for the next five weeks. The patient is measured for a set of custom lead shields that will be used during each treatment to protect the tissue and body parts surrounding the breast area from repeated exposure to X rays. Then the technologist carefully positions the patient on the treatment table, puts the shields on her body, and begins the radiation treatment. The patient feels no pain or discomfort, and 20 minutes later the treatment is complete.

The technologist now attends to another of her regular duties. She walks down the hall to the "hot" lab, where radioactive materials are stored. There, wearing special protective clothing, the technologist carefully loads radioactive cesium 137 into a tiny capsule. In the afternoon, a doctor will implant the capsule in a female patient's uterus to kill the cancerous cells of a tumor. The patient will then stay in a special isolated room, as she is literally radioactive. Usually the implant will be removed in a couple of days, and the patient can resume normal life.

Advances in Radiation Therapy

Although radiology and nuclear medicine have some significant differences, one unifying characteristic ties the two fields together—radiation. All of the diagnostic and therapeutic systems employed by radiologists and specialists in nuclear medicine utilize radiant energy in one form or another. One of the most significant findings in radiology research was the discovery that certain kinds of radiation are far more damaging to unhealthy cells, such as cancer cells, than they are to healthy cells. This finding led to the development of methods for delivering radiation to diseased areas on whatever scale of intensity

This 1926 etching by John Sloan shows two radiologists looking into the abdominal cavity of a patient through a fluoroscope.

and coverage might be required, ranging from the patient's entire body all the way down to precise locations a fraction of an inch in width.

In its early years, radiology was used mainly as a diagnostic tool and only in a limited way for actually treating diseases. In more recent years, however, radiology has come into its own as a tool for treatment, which doctors often refer to as intervention. What made this change possible was the introduction of a wide range of new devices that are used in conjunction with ordinary X-ray machines. Probably the most dramatic addition to the weapons of interventional radiology came in the late 1960s with the introduction of special X-ray-guided catheters by Drs. Charles T. Dotter and Melvin Judkins, radiologists at the University of Oregon Medical School Hospital. A catheter is a flexible hollow tube that a surgeon inserts into one of a patient's blood vessels or body cavities for the purpose of removing or inserting fluids. These special X-ray-guided catheters are now used in a diverse range of surgical procedures. They allow doctors to deliver doses of radioactive medicine very precisely to difficult-to-reach areas of the body.

Deciding When To Use Radiation Therapy

By far the most frequent reason for the use of radiation therapy is to combat cancer. Physicians and their patients hope that the waves of radiant energy will destroy the internal structure of the abnormal cells. At the very least, the radiation treatment should slow the cancer's development.

Radiation frequently is employed in conjunction with surgical removal of a tumor. After removal surgery, the purpose of the radiation is to destroy any remaining cancer cells in areas adjacent to the tumor. Radiation may also be used where a cancerous tumor is too far advanced to be cured by removal. In this case, the radiation reduces the size of the tumor and thereby diminishes pain, increases the patient's comfort, and improves his or her functional abilities.

As explained earlier, interventional radiation can be delivered either by an external source, such as an X-ray machine, or by means of an internal radioactive implant. The majority of radiation treatments involve using external beams of high-energy *ionizing radiation*, usu-

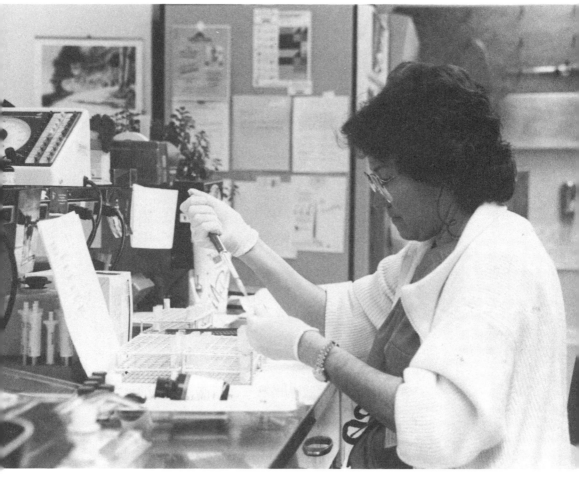

This laboratory technician prepares some of the tracer elements that will be detected by nuclear radiation scanning equipment.

ally X rays, directed to a carefully defined area of the body. External radiation is carried out only after an elaborate work-up, or preparation process, has been completed to locate precisely the treatment site, mask the surrounding area, and develop a proper dosage and treatment schedule.

Today, much of the external radiation therapy performed involves the use of the medium- and high-energy linear accelerator. This device greatly speeds up subatomic particles, such as electrons and X rays, and directs them at the treatment site. It is important to note that in using X rays to kill diseased cells, much more power is required to generate them than the X rays used for imaging. The linear accelerator can boost the power of X rays to the high energy levels required for therapeutic purposes. This machine has largely taken the place of an older device, the radioactive cobalt apparatus, which provided lower radiant energy levels and was more difficult to work with. The modern linear accelerator is a futuristic-looking machine, sleek and stream-lined. Though it can weigh up to several tons, the machine revolves easily on power-driven gimbals, or suspension devices, that allow the operator to deliver a beam of ionized radiation from almost any direction. The patient typically rests on a table below the machine in a room with lead-shielded walls to block the escape of stray rays.

Working from an outside control room, the operator delivers radiation to the treatment site in predetermined amounts, aimed at carefully plotted locations and angles. The patient has locator markings painted directly on his skin at the location to be treated, or on a plastic jacket that he wears. The linear accelerator then sends X rays to the diseased part of the patient's body. These rays routinely travel from several different directions to the same target. The purpose of this approach is to decrease the exposure of healthy body cells to radiation and increase the probability of killing the unhealthy cells, which are located at the point where the several beams converge.

Risks Versus Benefits

Almost every medical treatment involves some degree of risk, however small. One of the most important considerations that doctors and patients must address in deciding on how to treat a particular medical problem is that of measuring risks versus benefits. Are the potential risks of the treatment under consideration greater than the risks posed by the patient's present medical condition? They should not be. Are the potential benefits of the treatment greater than the known risks it involves? They should be.

It is a doctor's responsibility to seek a patient's informed consent before proceeding with any nuclear medical treatment. In other words,

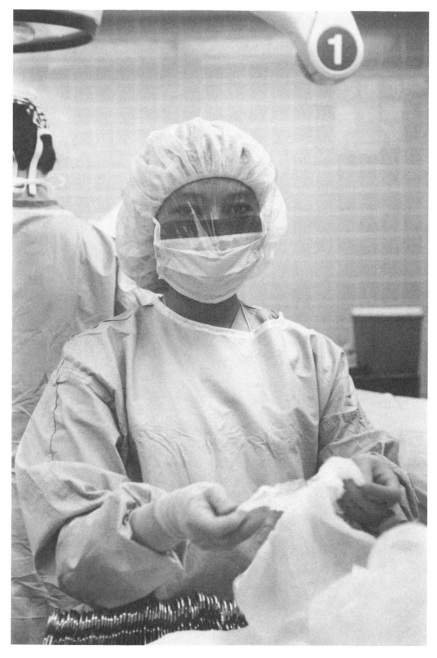

Working with radioactive materials requires special precautions on the part of medical workers.

the patient must understand what he or she is about to go through and must give the doctor permission to proceed. However, sometimes doctors assume patients will not understand the technical aspects of certain treatments. They may fail to explain fully some procedures to patients. It is in the patient's best interests to make sure that he or she is as informed as possible, and this may require him or her to ask the doctor questions. The patient should inquire about the nuclear treatment method the doctor is considering using, exactly how it will be carried out, what the risks and benefits are, and what alternative treatments exist, if any do, to accomplish the same results. Only when a patient has full information about all the pluses and minuses of the available options can he or she give a truly informed consent.

CHAPTER 5

RADIOLOGY DIAGNOSTICS

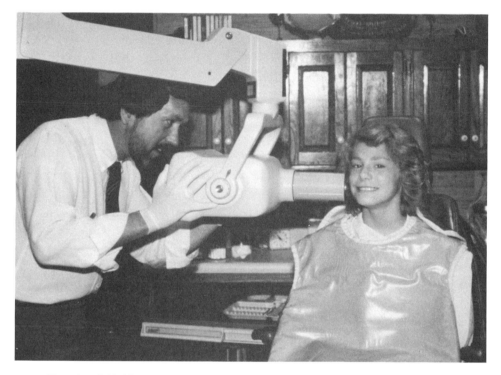

The dentist's X-ray machine is the one medical diagnostic tool using radiation that is familiar to millions of people.

Another scene, which happens nearly every day in many large hospitals, illustrates how radiology saves lives through quick and accurate diagnosis. In the middle of a quiet afternoon, the hospital intercom suddenly blares out loudly in all the corridors: "Code three, code three—all available medical personnel report to the Emergency

Room!" Among those who rush to respond is a radiology technologist. She learns that there's been a serious car crash, with several people injured. Her first patient is a teenage girl who is unconscious and moaning in pain. As she prepares to x-ray the girl, the technologist talks to her, as even unconscious people can be comforted by the sound of a friendly voice. The technologist then immobilizes the patient's head by surrounding it with sandbags. She takes several quick views of the girl's skull, with the machine on a high setting to compensate for any involuntary movements by the unconscious patient. After quick film processing, the picture shows a small skull fracture. A doctor immediately begins treating the patient, and the technologist moves on to the next crash victim.

The Modern Radiology Department

Radiology has come a very long way since that day in 1895 when Roentgen exposed his wife Bertha's hand to the emissions from a Crookes tube and made the world's first X-ray picture. The technology in today's radiology department is a match for that of any other medical technical discipline. The modern radiology department will contain an impressive array of state-of-the-art diagnostic and treatment devices made to the highest standards of precision and quality. Today, the modern wonders of radiology diagnostics include methods of intensifying images without increasing radiation dosages, the addition of a television system to show the body's internal functions in full motion, and the development of a range of contrast media, or dyes, that make it possible to image organs that were previously not visible in X-ray photographs.

Despite various alternative medical imaging devices that have been developed over the years, X rays still are very much an important part of the medical doctor's "tool kit." In fact, for certain diagnostic purposes, nothing can match the quality of information provided by a crisp, well-exposed X-ray picture. A conventional X-ray picture, employing sensitized film as a detector to reveal bodily structures, especially skeletal ones, is still the medical world's most often-used means of imaging the body's interior. In addition to showing the condition of bones, X rays are used to diagnose dental conditions, including cavities, and to detect lung and breast cancer. When a bone is x-rayed, the picture shows whether it is cracked or broken. A lung X ray will reveal abnormal conditions. A picture of the heart can reveal information about its size, shape, and positioning, all of which will aid in diagnosing a suspected heart condition.

Over the years, a great number of improvements have been made in both X-ray equipment and methodology. Modern X-ray tubes are capable of producing a high volume of exposures with proper density and clarity. Computers, when linked to radiology devices, can increase the quantity of and improve the quality of medical data. Modern film

Rembrandt's famous painting, the Anatomy of Doctor Tulp. *Before the advent of nuclear medicine, the only way that doctors could investigate diseases of the internal organs was to cut the patient open.*

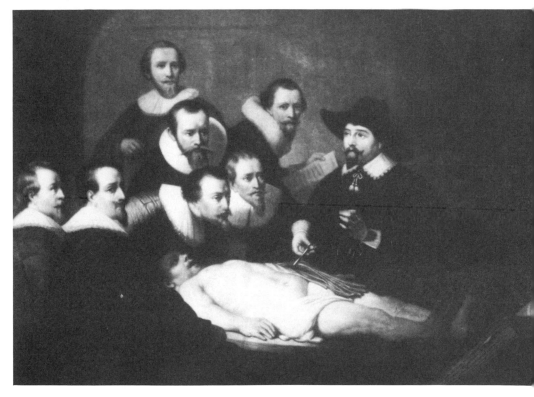

materials are able to reproduce details that are smaller than the human eye can see. The newest cassettes and holders designed to contain X-ray film are stronger and more protective, and make sharper registration, or visible imprint, of images possible. For example, according to Alan Ralph Bleich, formerly professor of radiology at New York Medical College, researchers found that they

> could increase the effect of the X rays on film by inserting fluorescent screens within the film holder. These were similar to the screens on which Roentgen had originally detected and discovered the X ray. The fluorescing [glowing] of screens, upon contact with X rays, in the form of the object being X-rayed, would intensify the effect of the X ray beam upon the film and greatly improve the resulting [pictures]. These intensifying screens are obtainable now in varying grades from slow to fast [degrees of sensitivity] and are part of the standard equipment of all X-ray laboratories.

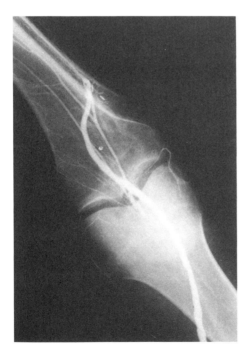

This X ray of a kneecap has been enhanced to show blood flowing through the arteries and veins.

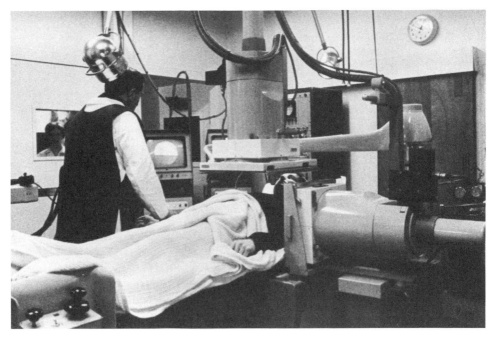

Modern X-ray equipment is often connected to television monitors to eliminate the time-consuming problem of film developing and permit more rapid diagnosis of health problems.

Among other improvements in equipment there are automatic film-developing machines that substantially cut the time required to develop a picture, from hours down to, in some cases, just minutes.

Denlul X Ruys

As anyone who has ever visited a dentist knows, dental X rays are used to study the teeth and jaw. The information in the pictures aids the dentist in detecting and treating conditions that could threaten the patient's teeth, gums, or general health. Dental X rays are taken when the dentist suspects that there might be problems in the teeth or the jaw tissue that are not visible in an ordinary examination of the mouth. When such problems are detected and treated early, unnecessary pain and permanent damage can be prevented. Typical of such problems are small cavities, technically known as caries, impacted wisdom teeth, cysts and tumors in the gums, and other oral conditions.

Modern dental radiology has dramatically improved the quality of X-ray images produced and at the same time reduced the quantity of radiation required to make them. In most cases, the picture is taken by placing the film behind the teeth, or by having the patient bite a tab that holds the film in position while the X-ray camera, positioned next to the cheek, makes an exposure. In the ideal modern dental situation, the small amount of radiation involved in such a diagnosis makes this one of the safest X-ray procedures.

Risk Factors and Accuracy of X Rays

There are two important considerations when deciding whether or not to get an X ray. The first is that every X-ray procedure carries with it some degree of exposure risk, however small. The other is that when a doctor, after careful consideration, orders an X ray, and it is performed by an expert technician using the latest low-dosage equipment and read by an experienced radiologist, the small risk involved in X-ray exposure is almost always outweighed by the value of the diagnostic information obtained.

To minimize radiation risks, people should avoid having routine X rays taken when there is no immediate, significant medical benefit. While this advice applies to people of any age, it is especially relevant to young people, who are at greater risk from radiation cell damage, particularly to reproductive organs, because their bodies are still developing and growing. In the case of pregnant women, the fetus should never be exposed to a routine X ray. For most X-ray procedures, a lead apron or similar radiation protection should routinely be worn, to shield uninvolved tissue and organs.

Everyone should be aware, too, that any radiography procedure involving a contrast medium being injected into the patient has the possibility of producing an allergic reaction. This can be anything from a minor itch or skin rash to unconsciousness and death. For this reason, all patients should be screened to learn whether they have a history of allergies; if they do, the dye must be tested on them for possible allergic reactions before it is injected. It should also be noted that when a contrast medium is used during an X ray, the effect of the rays on the cells is greatly magnified. This should be kept in mind by the radiologist, and appropriate dosage adjustments made.

The accuracy of X rays is another important consideration in radiology. Many radiologists and other medical persons describe the field of radiology as being an "art form." What they mean by this is that X-ray machines, unlike some medical devices, do not automatically give doctors neat, perfect information that allows them to make a diagnosis with a nearly 100% likelihood of being correct. Although X-ray machines, at their best, produce images that are wonderfully sharp, clear, and useful, these machines are not yet perfect imaging devices. There are several reasons for this. X-rays pictures, even those enhanced by a computer and contrast media, show the organs as patterns of less-dense and more-dense material. These images still fall far short of presenting full-dimensional, richly detailed visual information about live, functional body organs.

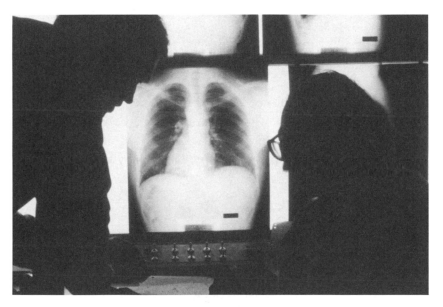

Two doctors examine a chest X-ray that clearly shows the lungs, heart, and abdominal organs.

This leads to the second and most important limitation of X rays. The information obtained by the use of even the finest X-ray equipment depends for its usefulness and effectiveness on the abilities of the technologist, the person who takes the picture, and also on the knowledge and skill of the radiologist, the person who interprets the picture. Radiologists are human like everyone else and therefore sometimes make mistakes. Some sections of the body look very much alike on X rays, rendering it difficult for the radiologist to make precise judgments. For this reason, reported X-ray results are not always as accurate as they could be. Alan Ralph Bleich sums up the problem of radiology being an art rather than a science, an art filled with difficult decisions and carrying a great deal of responsibility, saying:

> There are many places throughout the body where conditions simulate each other [look very similar]. Not only do they simulate each other in symptoms and complaint but also their X-ray findings may be somewhat similar. Differentiating one from the other represents experience, judgment, and reasoning faculties. The responsibility for arriving at the final decision weighs heavily upon the shoulders of the physicians concerned. This is especially true of the radiologist since his [or her] word on the interpretation of the [X-ray] films may determine the treatment of the case.

Therefore, when the results of an X-ray procedure have highly serious implications for the patient, the pictures should be read by several qualified persons. And if there are still any questions, additional X rays should be taken and interpreted at another radiology facility.

Fluoroscopy and Angiography

Fluoroscopy is the oldest of all the various forms of X-ray technology. It dates back to Roentgen's first skeletal viewing of his wife's hand on a screen of sensitized paper. By projecting a continuing, moving image on a fluorescent screen, the fluoroscopic X-ray technique shows many of the body's interior functions in motion picture action rather than as

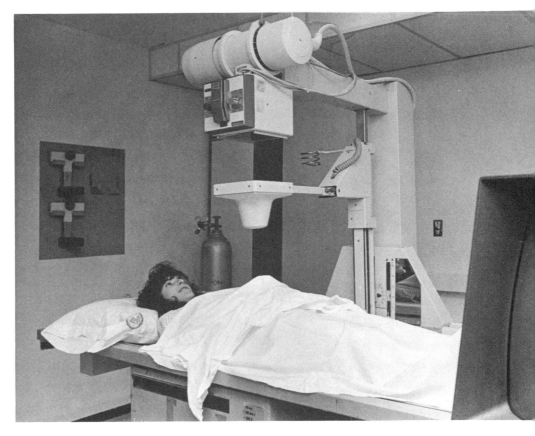

A patient awaits exposure to this modern fluoroscope.

a single frozen image; it therefore may be called for by a doctor when it is important to observe how a certain organ performs its activities. Today's fluoroscopic screens are significantly faster than those used in even the recent past. One bonus in this is that the use of high-speed screens reduces radiation exposure times, creating a safer working environment for both patients and operators.

Angiography is another useful component of the modern radiology department. An angiogram is one of the most important tools available to doctors today where diseases of the heart and blood vessels are concerned. Because of the varying abilities of X rays to penetrate different bodily materials, bones and lungs show up clearly on pictures whereas most other body organs, such as blood vessels, do not. In the angiography process, a dye is injected into the vessels to be examined, then a rapid series of pictures, a "movie," is immediately taken to show doctors the flow of the liquid through the blood vessels. The angiogram will reveal the functioning of all the system's parts, including the separate chambers of the heart, on X-ray film.

The angiogram is used in cases where the doctor suspects that the appearance of the heart's blood vessel channels may have been altered by a disease. One typical condition that alters normal heart operation is an aneurysm, a weakness in a blood vessel wall that allows ballooning of the vessel. Another is a narrowing or blockage of a vessel caused by either a fatty deposit, called an atheroma, or a clot, a clump of hardened tissue. One kind of clot, a thrombus, attaches to a vessel wall; another kind, an embolus, flows with the blood. Angiograms readily pinpoint all of these problems so that a doctor can promptly treat them. Angiography is also used to find changes in the normal patterns of the vessels that deliver blood to tumors or to body organs that have suffered injury. By evaluating any abnormalities detected in the patterns of these vessels, a physician may be able to judge the severity of the disease and decide on appropriate treatment.

One application of this technique is called carotid angiography. It is sometimes used with patients who have suffered symptoms of a stroke, a serious reduction of blood-flow to the brain, that have lasted fewer than 24 hours. The medical name for such an episode is a transient ischemic attack, or TIA. Here, the goal of angiography is to see whether the loss of blood-flow has been caused by a blockage in one of the carotid arteries, the major blood vessels on either side of the neck that carry blood to the brain. Another application is cerebral angiography, used when an aneurysm is suspected within the brain and before brain surgery to precisely visualize a tumor.

Angiography is also utilized to locate sites of narrowing or blocking in coronary arteries, those connected directly to the heart. The process is sometimes used in conjunction with catherization to remove the obstruction. In this and other related angiographic procedures, the contrast medium routinely is injected into the vessel under consideration through a catheter—in this case, a very thin, hollow plastic tube. To do this, the surgeon makes a tiny incision, or cut, in the skin above an underlying major artery, and then, guided by full-action X rays, moves the tip of the catheter through the artery to the site in the vessel where a blockage is suspected. The contrast medium is then injected, and a fast-sequence X-ray picture is taken of the flow. This will reveal any reduction in the flow caused by either a clot or the constriction, or squeezing together, of a vessel.

Depending on the location of the suspect site, an angiogram can take anywhere from minutes to several hours to perform. Risks associated with the procedure are an allergic reaction to the contrast medium and the possibility of physical injury caused by the catheter at the insertion site, within the vessel it is passed through, or at the site

These television monitors are connected to digital angiography equipment. In angiography, a dye that can make soft tissues visible is injected into a portion of the body. Soft tissues, such as blood vessels, are not easily seen with X rays.

of the dye injection. The future of this type of angiography is quite bright, particularly for interventional therapy.

Another type of angiography, digital subtraction angiography, or DSA, is one of a growing number of medical technologies that use the power of a computer to increase their performance abilities. An X-ray picture of the patient is taken before the injection of a contrast medium; a second picture is taken after the injection. The pictures are converted into digital, or number, code in a computer. When the unwanted information, fully identified in the first picture, is electronically subtracted from the second picture, the patient's blood vessels are clearly revealed by the contrast medium solution. This technique allows a doctor to see arteries and veins in full relief, or standing out visually, on an X ray, which unenhanced X rays cannot do.

Because of the increased clarity provided by the computer, DSA images usually require the injection of much less contrast medium than do ordinary angiograms. That makes this procedure somewhat safer, though there is a small risk of an allergic reaction associated with the use of the dye. Another advantage is that the catheter goes in only a short way, reducing the chances of the catheter causing injury from bruising or blockage.

Mammography and CT Scanning

There are many diseases that afflict members of one group with greater frequency than members of other groups. The groups may differ—for example, by race, by nationality, by occupation, by income, or by sex. For women, probably the most feared of such selective diseases is breast cancer. It is the most common cancer in women, with one in every 14 women developing it at some time in her life. Despite the many medical advances over the past century, including improved treatments for some kinds of cancers, the mortality, or death, rate from breast cancer saw little change until the early 1980s. That is when studies indicated that regular breast examinations for lumps and other cancer indicators, conducted by women themselves and by their physicians, could aid in early detection of the disease. At the same time, other researchers noted that when periodic breast X rays, or mammo-

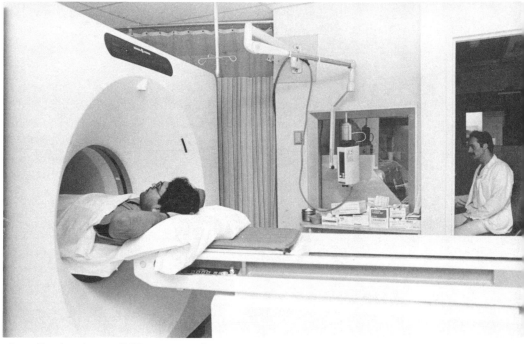

A patient enters a CAT scanner. Computerized axial tomography provides more accurate and more detailed images than conventional X rays.

grams, were given to all the women in a monitored test group, and treatment instituted when tumors were discovered, fatalities from the disease were reduced by 33%. A mammogram often can reveal a breast tumor long before it is large enough to be detected by hand examination, sometimes as much as two years earlier.

Using ordinary X-ray techniques, a small tumor in a deep-lying area of the breast would be more difficult to detect than one located near the surface. The mammogram compensates for this problem. Typically, the entire breast is first compressed between two horizontal plates on the mammography machine. This is done to equalize the breast's overall thickness. Then low-level X rays are passed through the breast and a picture taken on X-ray film to reveal any differences in tissue density. Because tumors and other growths consist of thickened, denser tissue, in a mammogram they will normally stand out from the surrounding healthy tissue as areas of white. Several views are usually taken.

Like many other diagnostic procedures, a mammogram by itself cannot reveal with 100% certainty whether the tissue under examination contains a malignant, or harmful, tumor. However, at present it is far and away medical science's most useful diagnostic weapon against breast cancer. For that reason, every woman should have a periodic mammogram at intervals suggested by her doctor. Recommendations are based typically on age, family history of cancer, and the patient's individual health profile.

Another radiological technique, *CT scanning*, is known by several names, including computer tomography, computerized axial tomography, and CAT scanning. CT scanning is another example of how computers have been joined with X-ray devices to create powerful new diagnostic systems.

CT scanning is quick and easy to do. In this process the patient lies within a circle of X-ray image detectors and the rays are delivered at varying angles to produce cross-sectional images of the body's interior. When all of these images are combined by a computer, they can be reproduced as a crisp two-dimensional image on a TV screen. Because CT scanning works with more information, it delivers far more detailed images than an ordinary X ray can. And CT scanning has other advantages. One is that the computer can manipulate the image to present from different angles the organ being studied. Also, because the computer is able to reinforce the X-ray image, less radiation has to be delivered to the patient.

Before the actual CT scan is taken, a doctor or nurse frequently gives the patient a contrast medium, either by injection or orally, in order to make the vessels or organs under consideration stand out better in the finished picture. The patient lies on a special table with a top that can be moved forward and back and up and down under remote electrical control by the radiology technician. The purpose of such movement is to accurately position the patient's body for the CT scanners. The CT scanner itself is a large machine with a tunnel or "doughnut hole" through its middle. Around the wall of the hole and pointing inward are many X-ray-beam projectors. The CT scanner machine can be tilted forward or backward by the technician to further aid in the precise aiming of the X rays.

The patient slides into the tunnel at a controlled rate, as though on a conveyor belt, and the doctor passes low-dosage X-ray beams through the body at intervals of only fractions of a second. A scanner rotates around the patient, recording what each beam "sees." The information from the scanner is sent to a computer, analyzed, and transformed into image "slices" on a TV screen—and, if desired, on film and videotape. The computer is able to clarify these pictures so that they are clearer than ordinary X-ray images. It can also combine adjacent views to create a three-dimensional image. The first CT scans, in 1972, were used to do brain scans, for which the technology remains particularly valuable. CT scanning is now used as well for imaging almost all parts of the main trunk of the body.

Magnetic Resonance Imaging

One of radiology's most useful tools, *magnetic resonance imaging*, or MRI, was first introduced in the late 1970s. The MRI procedure was formerly known as nuclear magnetic resonance, or NMR, but patients found the word "nuclear" so frightening that the name was changed. MRI produces three-dimensional images of organs and other structures within the body by means of electromagnetic waves rather than X rays. MRI uses a huge cylindrical electromagnet that surrounds the patient's body and exposes it to a strong, steady magnetic field 10,000 to 30,000 times stronger than the earth's magnetic field. Although powerful, this *electromagnetic field* is not known to be harmful.

MRI works in a unique and fascinating way. The magnet's attraction causes the nuclei of the hydrogen atoms in the water molecules in the patient's body to abandon their normally random positions and instead line up parallel to each other. When the MRI device sends a strong pulse, or sudden burst, of radio waves through the patient's body, the molecules' alignments are disrupted temporarily. The resulting fractured radio signals are picked up and sent to a computer that, by calculating the time it takes the signals to arrive, translates them into high-quality images.

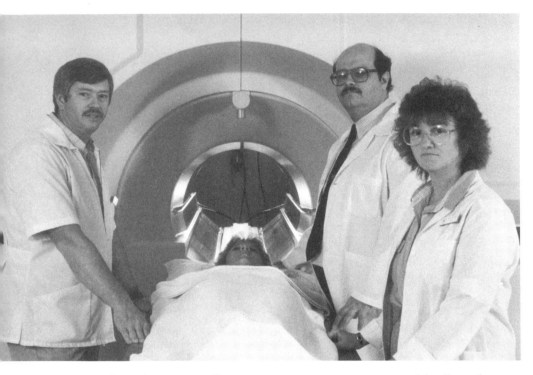

A nuclear magnetic resonance scanner uses a combination of magnetism and strong radio pulses to produce extremely sharp and detailed images of body tissues.

MRI allows images to be constructed in any body plane, that is, at any angle or thickness. It is especially useful for evaluating the state of the brain and spinal cord. It reveals a tumor with unmatched image quality and with a precise indication of its location and dimension. Abnormal fluid in the skull can also be detected. Other areas for which MRI delivers superior internal images are the eyes, ears, large blood vessels, heart, liver, spleen, pancreas, adrenal glands, joints—especially the knee—and, for some diagnostic purposes, the abdomen.

Although MRI is an expensive procedure at present, it is an extremely valuable one in certain situations. It has no known risks or side effects. Because it does not involve ionizing radiation, as X-ray procedures do, it can be performed many times on a patient without adverse effects. One drawback is that the MRI magnetic pulse is

A radiologist studies a series of magnetic resonance images, each one showing a different cross section of the brain.

capable of overriding a heart pacemaker's electrical signals and thus disrupting the heart's rhythms. So, persons fitted with a pacemaker should inform the radiologist ahead of time.

Ultrasound Scanning

Ultrasound scanning is also called sonography. Based on decades of use on many millions of patients, ultrasound scanning is considered to be completely risk-free for the patient. In this diagnostic technique, very-high-frequency sound waves are transmitted into the patient's body and their echoes picked up and analyzed to create an image. First utilized for medical purposes in the 1950s, ultrasound scanning was developed out of the naval sonar used for submarine detection during

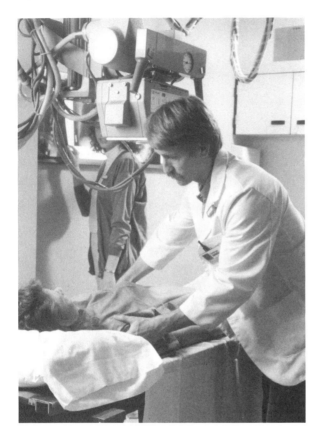

Modern X-ray equipment can appear quite frightening to patients, but the experience is painless.

World War II. The early ultrasound scanning images were single pictures, but most of today's scans are in the form of motion pictures. This makes it easier for doctors to study body functions.

An ultrasound scan is the simplest of all imaging procedures to carry out. The patient lies on an ordinary medical table and the ultrasound operator places a small hand-held device called a transducer on the skin in the area to be studied. The transducer contains a special crystal that converts inaudible high-frequency sound waves into an electric current that can be focused to take a picture of a wide, thin slice of body tissue. The transducer also acts as a receiver to pick up echoes of the sound waves, produced as they bounce off the boundaries of any internal organs and bones they strike. The echoes are processed electronically and converted by computer into motion picture images that

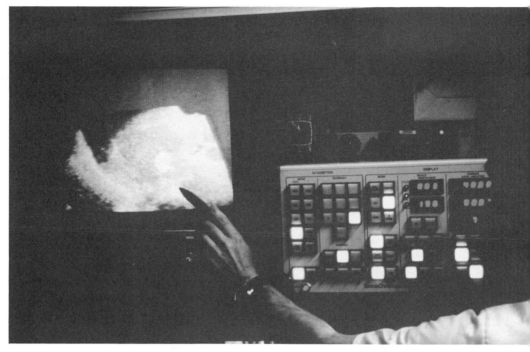

In a darkened room, a technician studies the image produced by ultrasound equipment.

are delivered onto a monitor screen. When the operator systematically moves the transducer along the skin, slices of the body's interior are shown progressively, or one after the other, on the screen.

The high-frequency ultrasound waves cannot pass through bone or gas, so the procedure does not have application in brain scanning (because of the skull) or for examining the lungs or intestines (which contain air). The sound waves do, however, travel readily through body tissue and fluids, which makes ultrasound scanning particularly useful for fetal monitoring during pregnancy. When it is used after about 16 to 18 weeks of pregnancy, the scan will show whether the fetus is growing at a safe and normal rate. In cases where the date of conception is not known, seeing the size of the fetus can give a reasonably accurate idea of the probable birth date as well.

Other information it may be possible to gain from an ultrasound scan includes whether the fetus has any gross abnormalities; the existence of congenital, or inborn, heart disease; the positioning of the placenta, the fluid-filled sack enclosing the fetus; and multiple fetuses. When members of the medical staff detect abnormalities, they can make appropriate preparations before delivery. If the doctor decides to perform an amniocentesis—withdrawal of amniotic fluid from the placenta for analysis—an ultrasound scan can help guide the insertion and proper positioning of the needle during the procedure. Analysis of amniotic fluid can reveal a number of fetal abnormalities; for example, Down's syndrome. Another scan may be done at a later date if there is reason to believe that the pregnancy is not proceeding normally. The doctor's concerns could include problems with the fetus's rate of growth, fetal movements that are absent or overly rapid, or problems experienced by the mother, such as vaginal bleeding. And in any pregnancy judged to be high-risk, a scan may be taken close to the time of birth to check on all conditions that could interfere with a successful delivery.

Following birth, a scan taken through the baby's anterior fontanel, a natural gap in the skull that gradually closes as the skull grows larger, can reveal several abnormalities, including tumors, hemorrhaging (serious bleeding), and hydrocephalus (fluid on the brain). Ultrasound is not ordinarily recommended for use on infants, but it is called for in many cases where a doctor suspects an infant has a significant health problem.

Another and highly specialized form of ultrasound scanning, echocardiography, is used to monitor the heart, a task for which it has become an important diagnostic resource. An expert analysis of the reflected ultrasound waves can reveal structural and functional abnormalities of the heart wall, valves, and major blood vessels. Blood-flow between chambers can be measured as well. The procedure's particular value is in aiding the diagnosis of heart valve disorders by revealing improper opening and closing. It can also reveal symptoms of congenital heart disease and such problems as heart muscle damage or enlargement, a potentially lethal weakening of the heart or blood vessel wall, and the existence of a blood clot within one of the heart's chambers.

The equipment and procedures for performing an echocardiogram are much the same as with other ultrasound scanning. The primary difference is in the interpretation of the scan results, which is performed by an appropriately trained cardiologist. These results, delivered as wavy lines on a special screen or on a paper tape, depict the structure of the heart and its functioning.

Doppler echocardiography, also known as angiodynography and Doppler ultrasound scanning, is a specific kind of ultrasound scanning used for looking at body systems in motion, such as blood coursing through veins. Doppler echocardiography can show a turbulence in the blood flow or the narrowing of vessel walls. The procedure makes use of the Doppler effect, which is the change in pitch of a sound that occurs when its source is in motion relative to the sound detector. Everyone has had the experience of hearing a train's whistle or a police car's siren rise in pitch as it comes closer and to fall in pitch as it moves away. This phenomenon is known as the Doppler effect. In the case of blood circulation monitoring, sound waves from a hand-held Doppler

A modern dental X-ray machine.

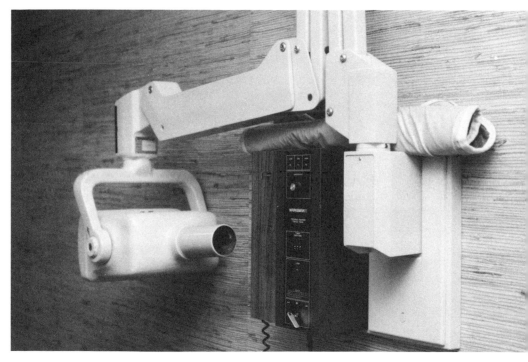

transducer strike moving red blood cells and the sound waves' frequencies change accordingly as the velocity of blood-flow changes. In other words, the device can distinguish between blood cells that move quickly and those that move slowly. Faster-flowing arterial blood shows up on the monitor in red, whereas slower-flowing venous blood appears in blue.

Thus, the radiology departments of modern hospitals are equipped with a wide range of dignostic devices. Radiological machines and techniques make it possible for doctors to discover, identify, and observe diverse problems ranging from bone fractures to breast cancer, from brain tumors to slow fetal growth and abnormal blood flow patterns. Using the information gained from these radiology tools, physicians can intelligently and, in most cases, accurately and safely administer the necessary treatments.

CHAPTER 6

CAREERS IN NUCLEAR MEDICINE AND RADIOLOGY

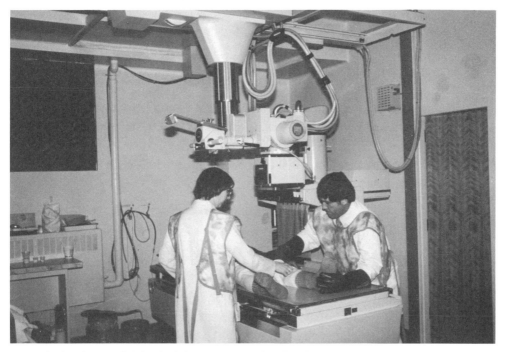

A doctor and a technician wear protective bibs as they prepare to x-ray a patient.

Many researchers who study the present career scene come to the same conclusion: the health care field offers many opportunities. This optimistic situation is likely to continue well into the future. One reason is that a growing number of older Americans require health services. Also, people both old and young are increasingly conscious of health care needs. The medical profession has made giant strides in its ability to keep people healthy, and people avail themselves of ever-expanding health care services. And if, as seems possible, some sort of national health care plan is enacted in the years just ahead, the need for trained health care professionals will become even greater. Two of the health specialties where opportunites are expanding at a dramatic rate are nuclear medicine and radiology.

In addition to receiving the considerable personal satisfaction of helping people in need, those who enter these fields make good livings. A report released by the American Medical Association in 1992 lists radiologists as receiving the second highest income of medical specialists, after surgeons. Thus these fields have been and continue to be attractive to young professionals entering the job market. However, it is wise for anyone interested in a career in nuclear medicine or radiology to examine carefully what these jobs entail before making any long-term professional plans or commitments. Following are descriptions of some of the most common jobs and duties performed in nuclear medicine and radiology.

Radiology Technologist

The actual taking of X-ray pictures is the job of the radiology technician, or RT, formerly called an X-ray technician. The RT's responsibility is to take the clearest, sharpest X-ray picture for diagnostic purposes while exposing the patient to the least possible radiation. Accomplishing these goals requires considerable skill. The RT must consider such technical variables as film density, contrast, sharp focus, and lack of distortion. Juggling these many factors and then making the right decisions requires skills that are taught in radiology technician school and then polished and perfected on the job.

The RT deals directly with people as well as with equipment. The technician must carefully consider the individual patient who is to be x-rayed—whether he or she is big-bodied or slim, heavily muscled or frail—because tissue thickness affects X-ray penetration. The RT

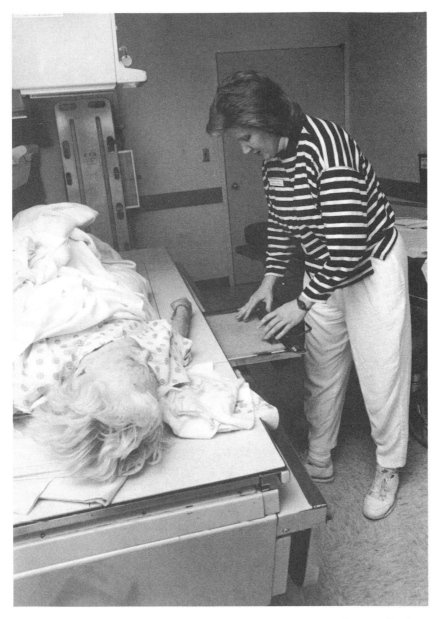

An technician inserts an unexposed negative underneath a patient as she prepares to x-ray the patient's hip.

positions the patient correctly for the scan, making sure he or she is comfortable. Next, before the picture is taken, the RT adjusts the distance of the X-ray device from the patient's body, then calculates electrical power settings and the length of the exposure. Although most of these considerations can be looked up in technical tables and charts, putting them all together in the right combination for each X-ray scan requires the best combination of training, experience, judgment, and a natural talent for the work.

Most RTs spend all their time performing basic X-ray scans, although some take additional training to do more advanced radiologic procedures, such as CT scanning and xeroradiography, which uses a special X-ray device and film to scan better pictures than conventional X rays. Xeroradiograms are especially useful when used in breast scans. Advanced RTs must also learn to use thermography, which does not work with X rays but instead uses highly sensitive heat detectors to locate tumors. This works especially well with breast tumors. Additional technologies are added to the field of radiology on a regular basis.

Radiation Therapy Technologist

The three-pronged counterattack that medicine can mount against cancer consists of surgery, chemotherapy, and radiation therapy. The responsibility for performing the hands-on work of radiation therapy is that of the radiation therapy technologist (RTT).

A doctor who is a specialist in cancer, called an oncologist, decides which form of treatment will be used with a particular patient. Usually, some combination of the three mentioned above will be utilized. It is common after the completion of surgery or a period of chemotherapy, for example, for a doctor to order several sessions of radiation therapy "just to be sure"—that is, to kill any stray cancer cells that might still remain in the patient's body. Almost 80% of cancer patients receive radiation therapy at some point in their illness. The treatment used might be radiation therapy with X rays or it might be some other form of radiation, such as radioactive radium implants. This decision will be made by the radiology department staff, usually by the chief radiologist, working with the RTT.

After the radiologist prescribes the radiation to be given, the day-to-day work of actually performing the radiation treatment is carried out by the RTT. Administering therapeutic radiation is significantly different from doing diagnostic X rays in that the dosage of radiation waves used in therapy is substantially more powerful than the dosage used in doing diagnostic X rays. Therapy-strength rays can cause harm if not properly delivered. Before treatment can begin, the proper settings for the X-ray machine or other type of radiation delivery system must be calculated using standard tables, training, and experience as guides. These calculations are performed by the RTT or, in some larger hospitals, by a medical physicist.

Once the radiation device is ready, the RTT positions the patient in a way that is comfortable and that will allow the rays to reach their target. The brain/spinal cord system, lungs and reproductive organs are particularly sensitive to radiation, so when they are involved, the RTT will create a treatment plan that protects those vital areas and keeps the radiation that reaches them to a minimum. Another way in which radiation is delivered to the target by an RTT is with radioactive implants. An implant is inserted inside the patient's body alongside the target, usually a tumor, then removed after a calculated length of time, when it has shrunk or destroyed the tumor.

Radiation therapy differs from diagnostic radiology in two key ways. First, getting a diagnostic X ray usually requires one quick session, whereas therapy can involve weeks of treatments, sometimes consisting of up to five sessions a week. Second, because the therapy patient is more often than not suffering from a life-threatening disease or condition, he or she probably is experiencing great emotional stress. The good RTT is sensitive to this fact and does everything he or she can to establish a bond of friendship and trust with the patient, and the patient's family as well. Not only does the reduction of stress make the radiation therapy experience an easier one for everybody, some medical experts say it can actually positively affect the eventual outcome of the illness.

Nuclear Medicine Technologist

A nuclear medicine technologist, or NMT, works with radionuclides. In doing an in vivo diagnostic procedure with a patient, the NMT administers, by injection or orally, a radioisotope specially formulated for safe use inside the human body. This material accumulates in a specific diseased tissue or organ of the patient. Then the NMT uses a special detector to measure—or a gamma ray camera or scanner to take a picture of—the radiation emitted by concentrations of the accumulated radioactive material. This information helps the doctor to understand better what is happening inside the patient.

The NMT also does in vitro testing by giving the patient a radioactive material and later collecting a sample of that patient's blood or urine and testing it. Or, in another diagnostic procedure called a radioimmunoassay, the NMT will take a sample of blood or urine from the patient and then mix it with a radioactive material. An analysis of this mixture can reveal with precision the presence and amount of various chemical and biological components of the fluid.

In addition to doing diagnostics, NMTs also use radioactive materials—or radiopharmaceuticals, as the drugs are called when used for therapy—to treat diseases. However, the radiation levels of radiopharmaceuticals are far higher than those of the materials used in diagnosis. As in diagnostic procedures, the drug is swallowed or injected. Once inside the body, the radiopharmaceutical circulates until it accumulates in the target tissue or organ. Its powerful rays will then kill diseased cells or fight other problems. Radio pharmaceuticals are typically prepared by specialists called pharmaceutists, who have additional training in safely handling, in administering, and in storing radioactive materials.

Diagnostic Medical Sonographer

Sonography, or ultrasound scanning, is performed by a technician called a diagnostic medical sonographer, or DMS. Most often, when a doctor prescribes an ultrasound for a woman during her pregnancy, it is not because she is having a problem but rather to make sure the fetus is developing normally. After doing an ultrasound of the fetus, the DMS consults a printed table that tells what fetal head size is normal for each age period. This information is invaluable in determining approximately how much time still remains before the woman will deliver, whether the fetus is suffering from certain defects, and whether it is still alive, if that becomes a question. Ultrasound is also used when doing an amniocentesis or fetal blood transfusion, where the technique provides precise guidance in positioning the hollow needle used in these procedures.

Sonographers are also called upon to perform ultrasound tests in areas of medicine other than obstetrics. When patients suffer unexplainable pain in the abdominal region, the DMS will scan the kidney, pancreas, liver, and other organs in search of tumors, cysts, or fluid

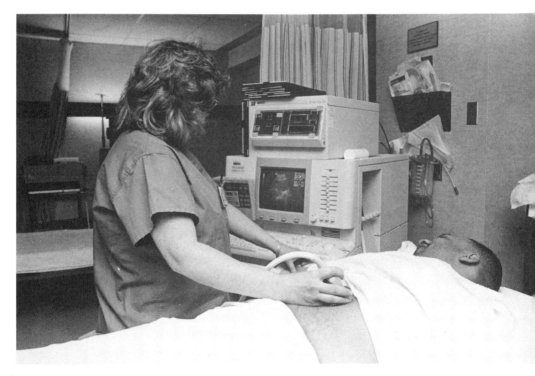

A medical technician administers a sonogram to a patient.

blockage. In gynecological investigations, those dealing with the female reproductive and urinary tracts, sonographers will make the same search in the pelvic region. Ultrasound examinations of the brain, to reveal tumors, and of the heart, to locate malfunctioning valves and chambers, are also part of a DMS's duties. So are sonograms of the eye, in search of certain kinds of physical or functional damage. Sonographers also perform sonograms to detect arterial and blood-flow problems.

Although their specific duties and work experiences vary, all of these nuclear medicine and radiology technicians, from RTs to sonographers, have certain things in common. First, they have been willing to commit themselves to the rigorous training required to be certified in these disciplines. They have also dedicated themselves to helping people with health problems that are often serious and difficult to deal with. And finally, these technicians are highly skilled professionals who take pride in their work.

CHAPTER 7

A LOOK INTO THE FUTURE

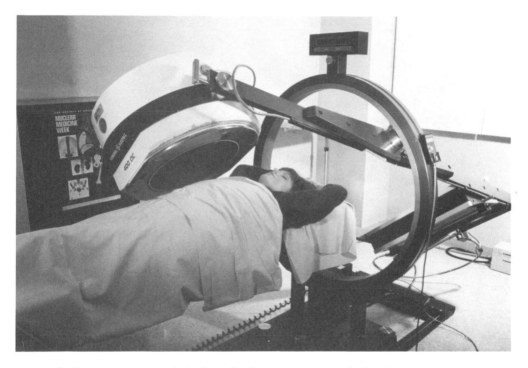

As the scanners and devices that use nuclear radiation become more sophisticated, earlier detection of illnesses is made possible.

The rate at which breakthroughs are coming about in medical technology is truly astonishing. Nuclear and radiological procedures are becoming increasingly diverse, complicated, and advanced. Although these improvements are made in the mechanical devices and chemical materials used in nuclear medicine and radiology, they lead to an increased understanding of how diseases develop and how the human body works.

The exciting fact is that advances in each of these areas has spurred on discoveries in the other. Sometimes such improvements have given doctors a better understanding of harmful diseases and how the human organism functions. And sometimes medical breakthroughs concerning certain diseases have revealed the need for new kinds of diagnostic or interventional devices. Fortunately, this sort of interactive advancement in both areas is likely to continue.

MRI Advances

Doctors have a great desire to improve their abilities to detect curable diseases early. The reason is simple: almost without exception, the earlier a disease is detected, the better are the chances for curing it. With heart disease, for example, or cancerous tumors, it has usually been necessary to wait for the condition either to cause noticeable symptoms in the patient or to become serious enough to be detectable by an imaging device. However, researchers have learned that many diseases cause chemical changes in the body before they are detectable. Future developments in magnetic resonance imaging are likely to make it possible for doctors to pick up these chemical changes early on, even at the microscopic level of cellular activity.

At present, MRI works only with the body's hydrogen atoms, but one day it may work with such elements as phosphorous and sodium as well. These elements, which magnetic devices will be able to detect, would be introduced into the bloodstream and then tracked. It would be possible, for example, to measure exactly how much damage a stroke or heart attack has caused or to detect and correct a clogged artery to the heart by measuring the quantity of phosphorous atoms in the heart muscle. It would also be possible to spot the crippling disease muscular dystrophy in its early stages with the aid, again, of magnetic resonance-scanned phosphorous atoms. Another future use for MRI technology will be in the diagnosis of tumors. By injecting magnetically detectable elements into a patient, an MRI scan could spot a tumor almost from its earliest moments.

MRI someday may let doctors learn in advance how healthy the organ of a prospective donor is. After the transplant, MRI may tell how well the donor organ is functioning. MRI also plays a role in the development of current drugs, which in time will advance medical knowledge and treatment. The technology helps researchers to penetrate the mysteries of the chemical world, making visible the structure of the chemical molecules. By analyzing the structure and doing experiments designed to make minute alterations—even moving individual atoms from one place to another in the molecule—pharmaceutical chemists work to invent even more effective therapeutic substances with fewer side effects.

Other Developing Technologies

In stereotaxic mammography, a fairly recent and still developing technology, a computer is used along with X rays to check on suspicious lumps in the breast. When a lump is suspected of being malignant, a needle biopsy, or tissue removal and examination, may be performed. This is done using a small hollow needle-probe. Guided by a computer that calculates the precise angle of insertion, the surgeon uses the needle-probe to withdraw a sample of the suspect tissue for an immediate examination. If a malignancy is found, surgery can be performed right away, rather than having the patient return days or weeks later after lab results have been analyzed.

A technique called microscopic ultrasound is not yet in general use. But researchers are working on an ultrasound device tiny enough to be inserted into an artery. It will be used to detect and measure the presence of blockages. The procedure will be performed simultaneously with a special type of surgery to remove any blockage. In the procedure, called an arthrectomy, a tiny high-speed drill inserted in the artery shaves away plaque, a fatty deposit that blocks the free flow of blood to the heart. Unable to see what they are doing, surgeons have had the problem of shaving away healthy tissue from the artery's wall. The new device, mounted right behind the drill, will spot plaque buildup with ultrasound, and its signal will be converted by computer to a continuous 360-degree picture of the artery's interior. With the tiny

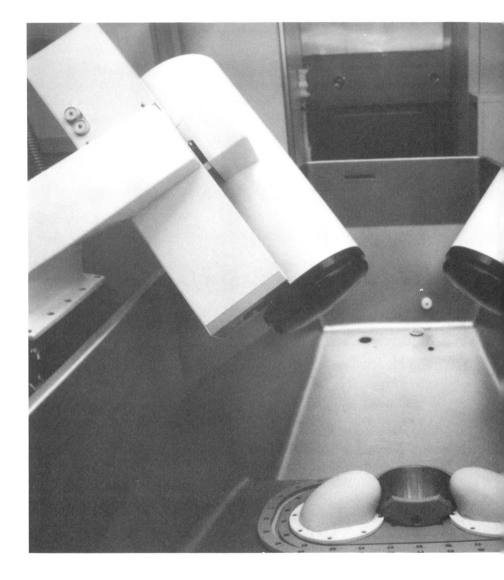

ultrasound device to guide them, doctors will be able to move the drill more accurately and remove much more plaque buildup without injuring the artery wall.

Other researchers are experimenting to develop ultrasound biopsy as a substitute for traditional surgical biopsy procedures. The tradi-

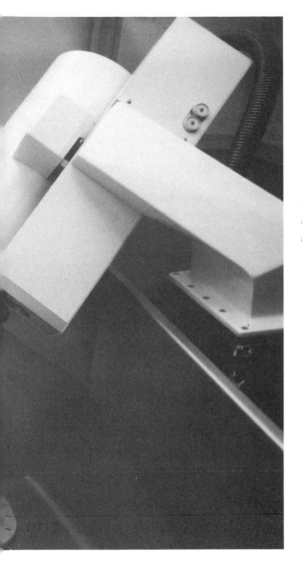

This lithotriptor uses high-energy shock waves to pulverize kidney stones without surgery.

tional biopsy involves the surgical removal of a small sample of tissue for study, usually to see if it contains malignant cells. An ultrasound biopsy would be noninvasive, that is, it would allow the doctor to gain the same information about the suspect tissue quickly and painlessly, without the need for surgically entering the body.

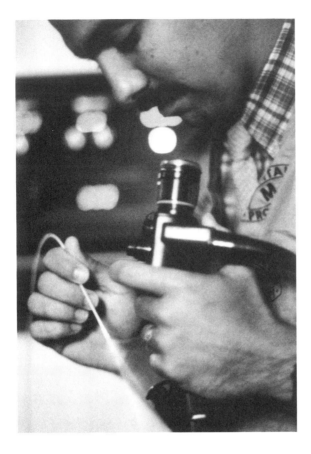

Laser light and fiber-optic cables are now used to look into areas of the body that previously could not be examined without difficult and hazardous surgical procedures.

Another new technology now in the early stages of development and use combines aspects of nuclear medicine with what doctors call monoclonal antibodies. These microscopic particles are made in the laboratory from genetically identical cells, all of which are capable of seeking out, reacting with, and neutralizing a single, specific antigen, or harmful foreign protein substance, in the human body. One of the most promising uses of monoclonal antibodies is in the detection and treatment of diseases associated with the appearance in the body of specific antigens. In other words, each disease has its own characteristic antigen. Theoretically, a monoclonal antibody that is specific to a certain cancer cell antigen could be tagged with, or attached to, a radioactive isotope. A patient would be injected with the radioactive monoclonal antibodies and after an appropriate waiting period, which might be several days, he or she would be placed under a gamma ray scanner and a picture would be taken of the body. Because monoclonal antibodies react only to one type of material—in this case, the antigens on the surface of cancerous cells of a tumor—they will cluster only where they find such cells. If the patient was tumor-free, no cluster would appear in the picture. The radioactive antibodies would then be quickly and naturally eliminated from the patient's body.

Much research is also being done on a lifesaving device called a nuclear cardiac heart pacemaker. Regular electric pacemakers, now in wide use, contain batteries and work by giving tiny rhythmic shocks to the heart to keep it operating properly. Surgery is required to implant

The new devices of nuclear medicine may look frightening, but they are far less dangerous than surgical procedures and in many cases provide the physician with more precise information.

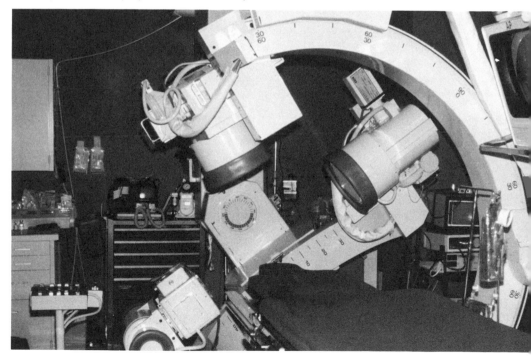

the pacemaker inside the patient's body, and when the batteries eventually run down, more surgery is required to replace them. Researchers are investigating the possibility of powering a pacemaker with radioactive material having a relatively long, active life. Instead of using a battery, heat given off by the radioactive material would be converted into electricity to operate the pacemaker. A number of engineering and medical problems still remain to be solved before a nuclear-powered cardiac pacemaker can be put into safe use, but the possibilities look good.

Continuing research into new techniques in nuclear medicine and radiology offers hope for great advances in health care. In the 21st century, it is likely that both diagnosis and treatment of diseases and harmful medical conditions will reach new and unheard-of levels of speed, accuracy, and effectiveness. The result is bound to be increasing numbers of people living longer, healthier, and happier lives.

APPENDIX:
FOR MORE INFORMATION

The following is a list of organizations and associations that can provide further information on the issues discussed in this book.

American Board of Radiology (ABR)
2301 West Big Beaver Road, Suite 625
Troy, MI 48084
(313) 643-0300

American College of Radiology (ACR)
1891 Preston White Drive
Reston, VA 22091
(703) 648-8900

American Roentgen Ray Society (ARRS)
1891 Preston White Drive
Reston, VA 22091
(703) 648-8992

American Society of Radiologic Technologists
15000 Central Avenue SE
Albuquerque, NM 87123
(505) 298-4500

Radiological Society of North America (RSNA)
2021 Spring Road, Suite 600
Oak Brook, IL 60521
(708) 571-2670

Society for Diagnostic Medical Sonography
270 Coit Road, Suite 508
Dallas, TX 75251
(214) 239-7367

Society for Nuclear Medicine
136 Madison Avenue, 8th floor
New York, NY 10016
(212) 889-0717

COLLEGE OF THE SEQUOIAS
LIBRARY

FURTHER READING

Caulfield, Catherine. *Multiple Exposures: Chronicles of the Radiation Age.* New York: Harper & Row, 1989.

Clayman, Charles B., ed. *The American Medical Association Home Medical Encyclopedia.* 2 vols. New York: Random House, 1989.

―――. *Diagnosing Disease.* Pleasantville, NY: Reader's Digest, 1989.

―――. *Fighting Cancer.* Pleasantville, NY: Reader's Digest, 1991.

Dewing, Stephen B. *Modern Radiology in Historical Perspective.* Springfield, IL: Charles C. Thomas, 1962.

Eisenberg, Ronald L. *Radiology: An Illustrated History.* St. Louis, MO: Mosby-Year Book, 1991.

Galton, Lawrence. *Med Tech: The Layperson's Guide to Today's Medical Miracles.* New York: Harper & Row, 1985.

Lillie, David W. *Our Radiant World.* Ames, IA: Iowa State University Press, 1986.

Nassif, Janet Zhun. *Medicine's New Technology: A Career Guide.* New York: Arco, 1979.

Pinckney, Cathy, and Edward R. Pinckney. *The Patient's Guide to Medical Tests.* 3rd ed. New York: Facts On File, 1986.

Pringle, Lawrence. *Radiation: Waves and Particles, Benefits and Risks.* Hillside, NJ: Enslow, 1983.

Shtasel, Philip. *Medical Tests and Diagnostic Procedures.* New York: Harper & Row, 1990.

Time-Life. *Fighting Cancer.* Alexandria, VA: Time-Life Books, 1981.

———. *How Things Work: Medicine.* Alexandria, VA: Time-Life Books, 1991.

GLOSSARY

alpha particles charged particles emitted from the nucleus of a radioactive atom

atom the smallest unit of an element; it consists of a nucleus orbited by electrons

beta particles high-energy electrons given off by radioactive atoms

CT scan computer tomography; a special type of X-ray procedure in which rays are sent from many angles through a target; detectors on the opposite side measure the degree of absorption, and the information is then translated by computer into a picture

electromagnetic field an effect produced when electric and magnetic forces interact within a space

electron a negatively charged particle that orbits the nucleus of an atom

fluoroscopy an X-ray procedure performed by a device that continuously emits X rays to produce moving pictures of the inner workings of its target

gamma rays highly penetrating emissions given off by some radioactive materials

ionizing radiation rays powerful enough to knock electrons free from the nucleus of an atom or even disrupt the atom's nucleus; used to kill diseased body cells

magnetic resonance imaging (MRI) a scanning procedure that uses radio waves emitted in a powerful magnetic field to create detailed images of organs and other internal structures; its diagnostic applications are similar to those for CT scanning

nuclear medicine the field of knowledge that uses an ionizing radioactive source within the patient's tissue or organs to produce images or treat diseases

positron emission tomography (PET) a nuclear imaging procedure that allows doctors to view the chemical and biological processes of the body in a motion picture

radioactivity a phenomenon occurring naturally in some elements where the nucleus undergoes continuous powerful changes and emits particles; the phenomenon can be brought about artificially as well

radiology the field of knowledge that uses ionizing and nonionizing radiation for medical diagnosis and treatment

radionuclides radioactively unstable versions of normal elements that are injected into a patient's bloodstream and then traced using gamma ray cameras, PET scanners, or SPECT scanners

single photon emission computer tomography (SPECT) a nuclear imaging procedure that creates a three-dimensional image of the interior of the body

ultrasound sonography; in this technique, very-high-frequency sound waves are transmitted into the patient's body and their echoes are picked up and analyzed to create an image

X rays ionizing radiation of short wavelengths that can penetrate certain solids; the depth of penetration is a function of the radiant power of the rays

INDEX

Wendy and Jack Murphy have worked as freelance writers for more than 15 years. Wendy, a former senior editor at American Heritage, has written extensively for Time-Life Books and *Reader's Digest*, including a number of volumes on a broad range of medical topics. She is also the author of medical works written in collaboration with physicians, as well as articles created for professional magazines. Jack is a writer on high-technology topics and is the author of several popular-audience technical books.

Dale C. Garell, M.D., is medical director of California Children Services, Department of Health Services, County of Los Angeles. He is also associate dean for curriculum at the University of Southern California School of Medicine and clinical professor in the Department of Pediatrics & Family Medicine at the University of Southern California School of Medicine. From 1963 to 1974, he was medical director of the Division of Adolescent Medicine at Children's Hospital in Los Angeles. Dr. Garell has served as president of the Society for Adolescent Medicine, chairman of the youth committee of the American Academy of Pediatrics, and as a forum member of the White House Conference on Children (1970) and White House Conference on Youth (1971). He has also been a member of the editorial board of the *American Journal of Diseases of Children.*

C. Everett Koop, M.D., Sc.D., is former Surgeon General, deputy assistant secretary for health, and director of the Office of International Health of the U.S. Public Health Service. A pediatric surgeon with an international reputation, he was previously surgeon-in-chief of Children's Hospital of Philadelphia and professor of pediatric surgery and pediatrics at the University of Pennsylvania. Dr. Koop is the author of more than 175 articles and books on the practice of medicine. He has served as surgery editor of the *Journal of Clinical Pediatrics* and editor-in-chief of the *Journal of Pediatric Surgery.* Dr. Koop has received nine honorary degrees and numerous other awards, including the Denis Brown Gold Medal of the British Association of Paediatric Surgeons, the William E. Ladd Gold Medal of the American Academy of Pediatrics, and the Copernicus Medal of the Surgical Society of Poland. He is a chevalier of the French Legion of Honor and a member of the Royal College of Surgeons, London.

PICTURE CREDITS

Betts Anderson/Unicorn Stock Photos: pp. 63, 83; Argonne National Library: p. 31; J. Bisley/Unicorn Stock Photos: p. 85; Jeff Kaufman/FPG International: cover; Martha McBride/Unicorn Stock Photos: pp. 96–97; Tom McCarthy/Unicorn Stock Photos: p. 93; © Mike Matthews: pp. 13, 41, 48 (top and bottom), 59, 61, 66; National Cancer Institute, National Institutes of Health: p. 81; National Library of Medicine: pp. 16, 18, 19, 21, 26, 27, 29, 33, 34, 37, 39, 43, 52–53, 57, 65, 67, 69; © Martha Tabor/Working Images Photographs: pp. 44–45, 87; Unicorn Stock Photos: p. 99; Terry Wild Studios: pp. 55, 73, 78, 79, 80, 98; Shirley Zeiberg Photo: pp. 71, 75, 91.